SING AND PRAY AND SHOUT HURRAY!

Compiled by
Roger Ortmayer

Friendship Press
New York

Acknowledgments

Editor's Note: This collection is representative of worship materials from the world over. Most of the items are traceable to a known source and are credited below. Other items are, in the words of the compiler, "fugitive in nature," developed for special occasions, but never formally printed or copyrighted. To writers, composers and poets of all such "fugitive" items we state our thanks asking that if they inform us of their authorship we will acknowledge them in a future edition.

PP. 4, 16, 62, songs from *New Songs of Asian Cities*. Published by the Urban and Industrial Mission Committee of the East Asia Christian Conference, 1972.

P. 21, song from *Heavy Hymns*. Published by Agape, Carol Stream, Ill. © 1972 by Summerlin Music.

P. 24, "Experimental Form of Worship" from *The Guardian*, December 22, 1971.

PP. 28, 30, 31, "Ecumenical Act of Thanks," "United Service" and "Sunday Worship" by permission of I-to-Loh and the East Asia Christian Conference.

P. 38, "Political Involvement" reprinted by permission of *The Guardian*.

P. 40, "To the Westerners" by Shanmugha Subbiah in *Kurukshetram*, a collection of essays, stories and poetry, Madras, 1968. Copy here reprinted from *Salvation Today*, published by the World Council of Churches.

P. 44, "Answer to the Question from Our Left-Wing Friends on Why We Pray" from *Risk*, Vol. V, Nos. 3 & 4, 1969, pp. 36-38.

P. 45, "Prayer" by Halina Bortnowska from *Salvation Today and Contemporary Experience*, published by the World Council of Churches, Programme Unit on Faith and Witness, Commission on World Mission and Evangelism.

P. 46, "Friendship" from *Worship in Youth's Idiom*, Ecumenical Christian Centre Publication, Bangalore, India.

P. 49, "Unity in Diversity" by Roger Ortmayer. Used by permission of the author.

P. 50, "Good-bye" from *Risk*, Vol. VII, No. 3, 1971.

PP. 51, 52, 53, 54, poems "The Traps," "Drop-Out," "Lord, I am Twenty-five!" and "The Thief" by Mrs. Vimala Manuel. Originally done for the Committee for the Dutch Churches. Courtesy of Lesslie Newbigin, Bishop in Madras.

P. 55, "Latin American Lord's Prayer" by Mario Benedetti from *Inventario*, Ediciones Alfa, Montevideo. Copy here reprinted from *Salvation Today*.

P. 56, "Lament for the June Sun" by Abdul Wahab al-Bayati from *Encounter*, October 1971, Vol. XXXVII, No. 4, translated by Besmond Stewart. Copy here reprinted from *Salvation Today*.

PP. 57, 58, Personal prayers from "School on Worship" in Bangalore. From *Worship in Youth's Idiom*, Ecumenical Christian Centre Publication, Bangalore, India.

P. 59, song from *Persian Hymnbook*, 1969.

P. 60, song provided by the World Council of Churches.

P. 61, song from *Sing a New Song*. St. Catherine's Home, Andheri, Bombay 58 AS. All rights reserved.

P. 63, song from *Sing Again, Africa!* © 1970 Galliard Ltd., New York.

<u>Photo Credits</u>

P. 12, World Council of Churches

P. 22, "Mary and the Child Jesus." Artist unknown, photo by Arno Lehmann.

All other photos by John P. Taylor, World Council of Churches.

Library of Congress Cataloging in Publication Data

Ortmayer, Roger.
  Sing and pray and shout hurray!

  Bibliography: p.
  1. Worship programs.   2. Prayers.   I. Title.
BV198.O77   242'.8   74-3074
ISBN 0-377-00004-3

Copyright © 1974 by Friendship Press, Inc.
Printed in the U.S.A.

Contents

4 Song: "O Sing Unto the Lord a Song That's New"

Preclusive
6 The Experience of Liturgy and Prayer and Song

Fragments... Miscellany
16 Song: "The World Is Upside-Down"
18 Four Events — Yushi at Bangkok
20 Salvation in the Midst
21 Song: "Salvation"
23 Christmas Message

Liturgies — United in Prayer
24 Experimental Form of Worship (India)
26 African Service
28 An Ecumenical Act of Thanks (Argentina)
29 Song Poem: Thank You, Lord
30 United Service: Roman Catholic and Protestant Christians Together (Taiwan)
31 Sunday Worship (Taiwan)
32 A Liturgy for Pentecost (Switzerland)
38 Political Involvement (India)
40 Poem: To the Westerners
41 Conference on "The Unmasking of Man: Marx or Freud" (Germany)
44 Answer to the Question from Our Left-Wing Friends on Why We Pray (Germany)
45 Prayer (Czechoslavakia)
46 Friendship (India)
47 African Eucharist: Processional Hymn
49 Unity in Diversity: Worship from World Conference on Salvation Today (Thailand)
50 Poem: Good-bye

A Handful of Prayers
51 The Traps
52 Drop-out
52 Lord, I Am Twenty-five
54 The Thief
55 Latin American Lord's Prayer
56 Lament for the June Sun
57 Short Prayers

A Clutch of Song
59 From Persia
60 Con Xom Lang
61 There Are Numerous Strings
62 Let's Grow
63 Ama Xhe Sha

64 **Helpful Resources**

O Sing Unto The Lord A Song That's New

Music: Sixter David Marie
Text: Fred Kaan

O sing to the Lord a song that's new. He has done what the world cannot do. His arm is strong, cre-a-tive his will. By his voice the storm is stilled.

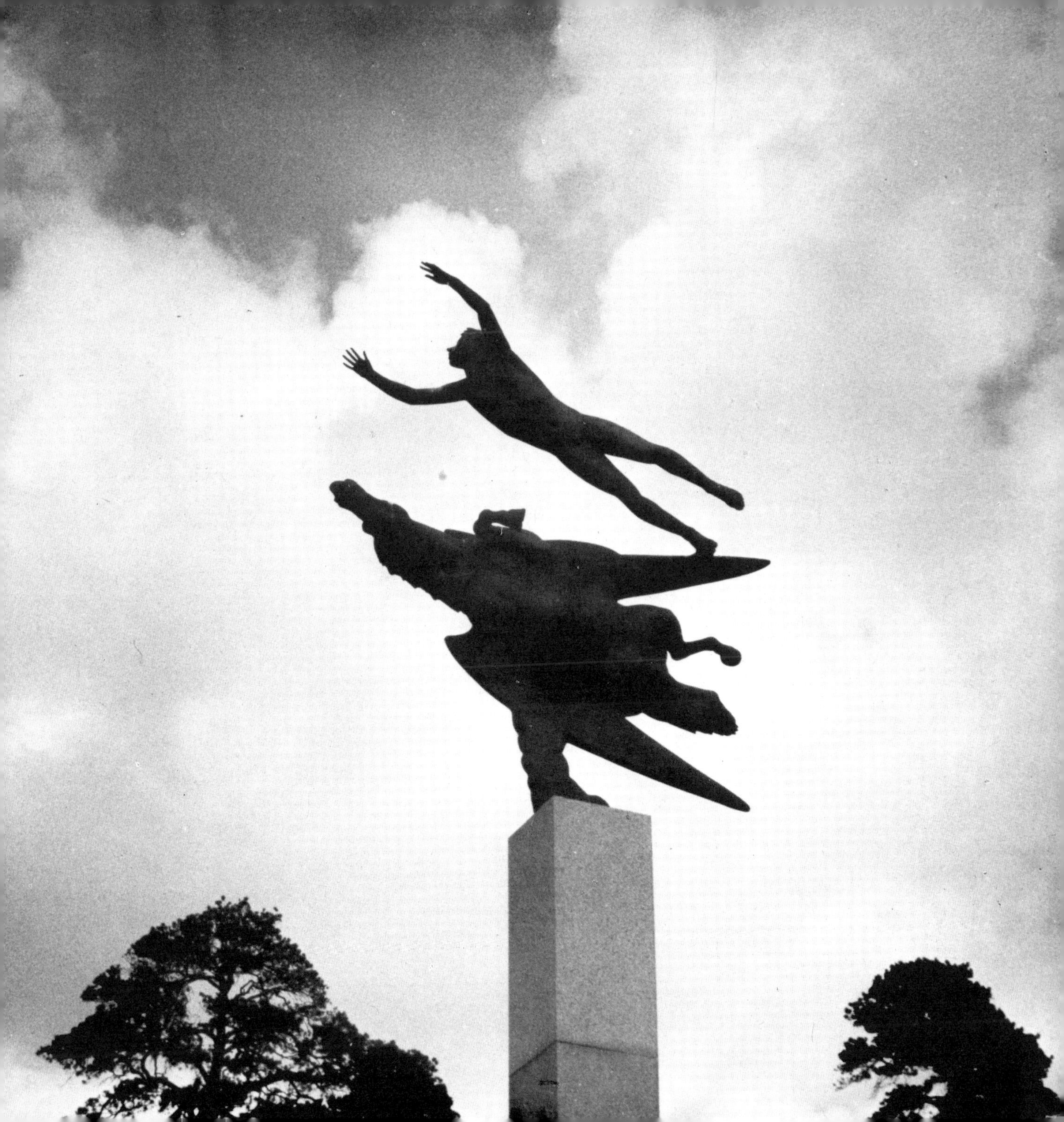

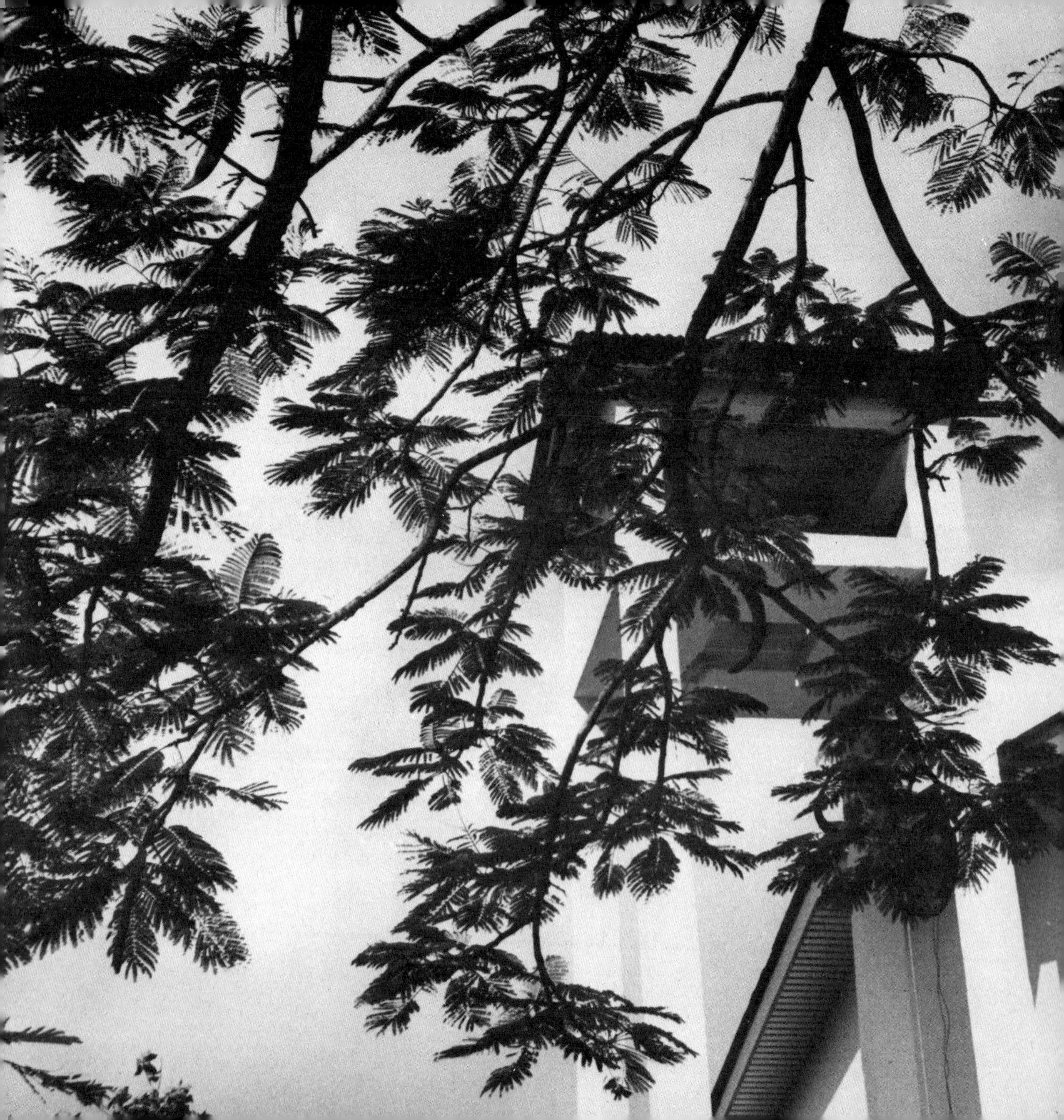

Preclusive

The Experience of Liturgy and Prayer and Song

In worship and prayer we ask for the Holy Spirit, the giver of new life. This is why old forms can suddenly come alive in quite unexpected ways, and new forms can emerge.

In a church in Jerusalem they do a service of St. James and it is so old it seems new. On Mt. Athos I spent a week trekking the rock paths from monastery to monastery, and before the sun came up each morning the monks would whack an oak beam and a heavy iron triangle and the sound seemed the sound of another world (though it was wood and cast iron). I got up and went down to church and it was another world—a dim and tentative morning light making faint the Christos in the dome, the monks lighting and blowing candles and reading and chanting. The frescoes were more than a backdrop: they were a presence—*the company of saints.*

And on Trafalgar Square, Sunday, April 8, 1973, I took the bread of *his body* and the Bishop of Damaraland-in-exile and brown cassocked monks and gray sisters and gradually, when freed-up, the housewives and counselors and students and preachers danced in joy about the square.

Dance then wherever you may be
I am the Lord
of the dance said he
And I'll lead you all
wherever you may be
I'll lead you all
in the dance said he.
    Sidney Carter, "Lord of the Dance"

Down the street, in St. James Picadilly (bless you, Christopher Wren) Dutch-born, German jazz composer and band leader Peter Janssens led his group in a wondrous jazz prayer written by a revolutionary Nicaraguan priest (Ernesto Cardenale), an intercession for actress Marilyn Monroe.

If you don't worship then *Lord, have pity on your soul* (like they say about those who are dead . . . or dying . . .).

Right now there is no "correct" way to worship the Lord; no such thing as sacred music exists; hardly any religious symbols can be recognized. . .
but people do sing praise
    and pray
    and cry hurray . . .
and they congregate to sing praise
    and pray
    and cry hurray . . .
    and
    ask for justice
    seek liberation
    break bread
    drink wine.

I am happy
because You have accepted me,
dear Lord.
Sometimes I do not know what to do
with all my happiness.
I swim in Your grace
like a whale in the ocean.
The saying goes:
"An ocean never dries up,"
but we know
that Your grace also never fails.

Dear Lord,
Your grace is our happiness.
Hallelujah!
(a young African)

A line, a shade, a color—
their fiery expressiveness.
(Dag Hammarskjöld)

It may be that we work at ritual building in the wrong way. We tend to make a word liturgy and then look around for those who can do it. If we don't have an organist, a dancer, an actor person, we go broke.

How about starting with gifts? Someone plays a musical saw and another mimes. That's enough to get going.

Westerners laid heavy burdens on converts in other continents—baroque music and eighteenth-century rhetoric. But now it is the second and the third generation of Christians and they are getting liberated to their own cultural and inner rhythms and pulses—their own idiom. Some of it may not be exportable, and some untranslatable . . . and even the best of translations are but approximate.

Still, the mix is good. A Sikh scholar, now a Bombay journalist, told me recently that jazz is the first really international language. He says he enjoys every continent and is at home everyplace because he loves jazz. He may be correct; the rhythm, just now, may be more important than the idea.

The art of worship is many arts . . . sound, sight and touch, separately and in mix.

Some three centuries of rationalism in Western Christendom has promoted audio arts to the detriment of the visual and almost obliterated the kinesthetic. Even such a simple act as the *kiss of peace* is awkward to most Western congregations, to say nothing about dancing together.

How can you sing a calypso rhythm without moving your body? and laughing? or pray the Latin American version of the Lord's Prayer without sorrow? or see the mother and child without joy?

"Go search everywhere to the highways and the byways and force them to come in. My table must be filled before the banquet can begin."
(Luke 14:23)

"Where two or three are gathered together, in my name. . . ."
(Matthew 18:20)

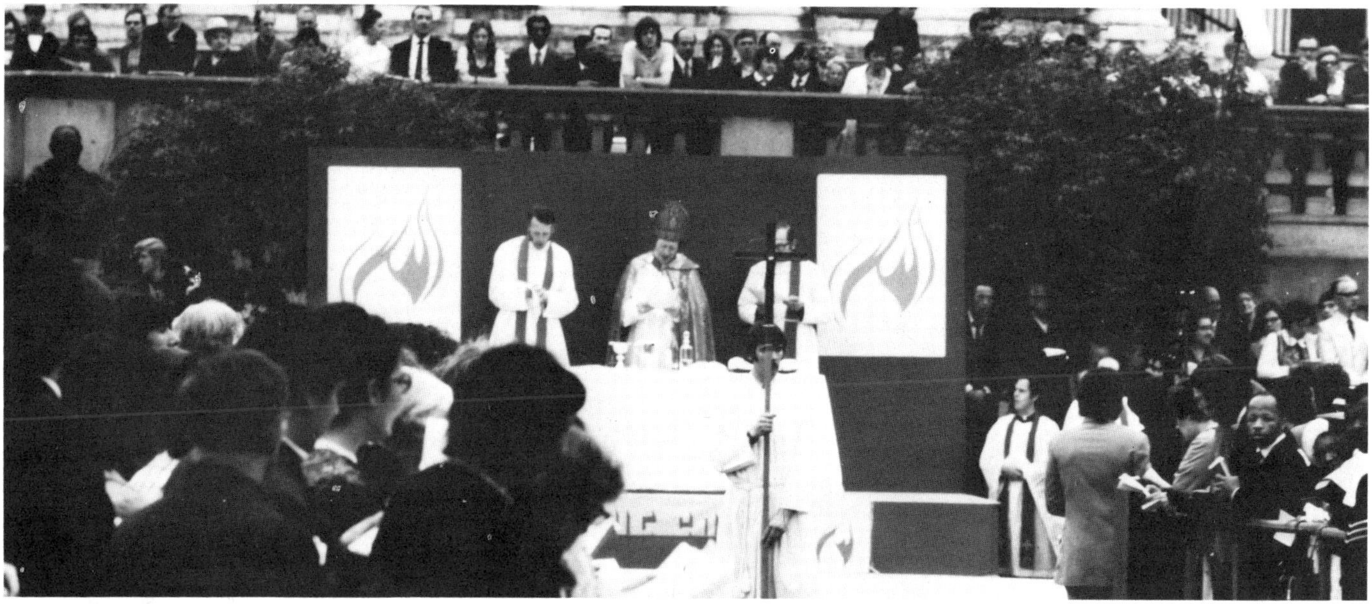

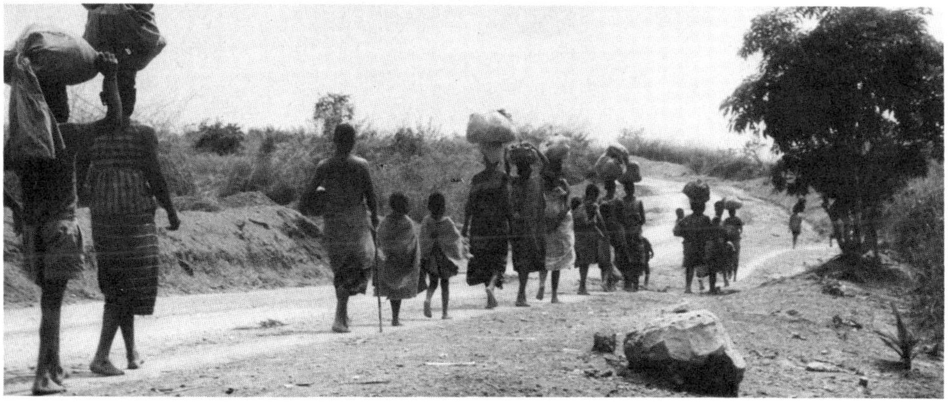

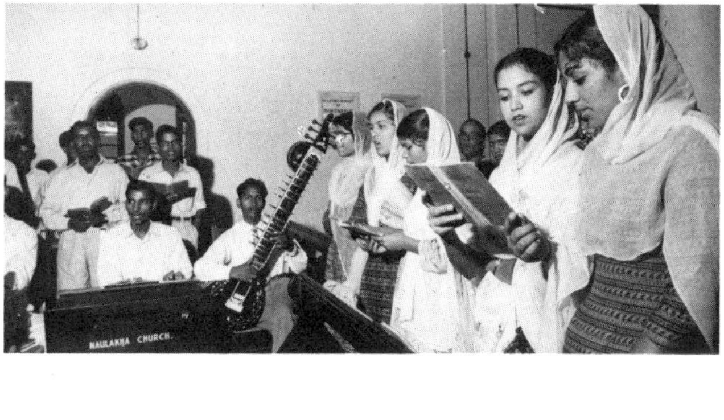
NAULAKHA CHURCH.

Perhaps today will begin to show the way. At any rate we can be sure that we are part of something which Christ is doing throughout his church across the world from the Missa Creolle to the songs of Père Du Val, from the freedom songs cradled in the American South to Dunblane praises, from "let's play a game" to "sing 'round the year." And what we start today may—who knows?—send ripples 'round the earth as Christ makes all things in his creation new.

Worship is too precious to be left to the performances of religious professionals. Lay persons are also professionals: sculptors, mechanics, actors, poets, nurses, musicians, singers, architects, dancers, doctors, teachers, students. . . .

And some are socialists, some are politicians, capitalists, prisoners, rebels and status "quoers" . . . .

Most should be theologians, and it is great to have the help of those professionals whose life is given to reflecting on the things of God.

The wonder of worship today is any worship at all . . . the wonder is that it is breaking out all over in about every land and in all tongues and in idiom marvelous. Of course, much is strained and some is awkward and lots of what is going on will never be heard of again. That's okay. We learn nothing by not trying, testing.

Worship is the heart of Christian action. Its reform is urgent. And its reform is impossible unless Christians tackle with a new courage the fundamental questions which in the religious East or the secular West now challenge their central doctrines.

Surprised by joy!
(C. S. Lewis)

Then—
Lo! lo and behold!
The unexpected works—
so beautiful!
so awe striking!

and maybe (just as astonishing)
          so subtle. . .
          so comforting. . .
          so. . . .
Awake!
    Sing!
        Pray!
            Meditate!
                Act!
      (i.e. *celebrate!*)
          —Roger Ortmayer

**No single event can awaken
within us
a stranger totally unknown
to us.
To live is to be slowly born.**
(Antoine de Saint Exupéry)

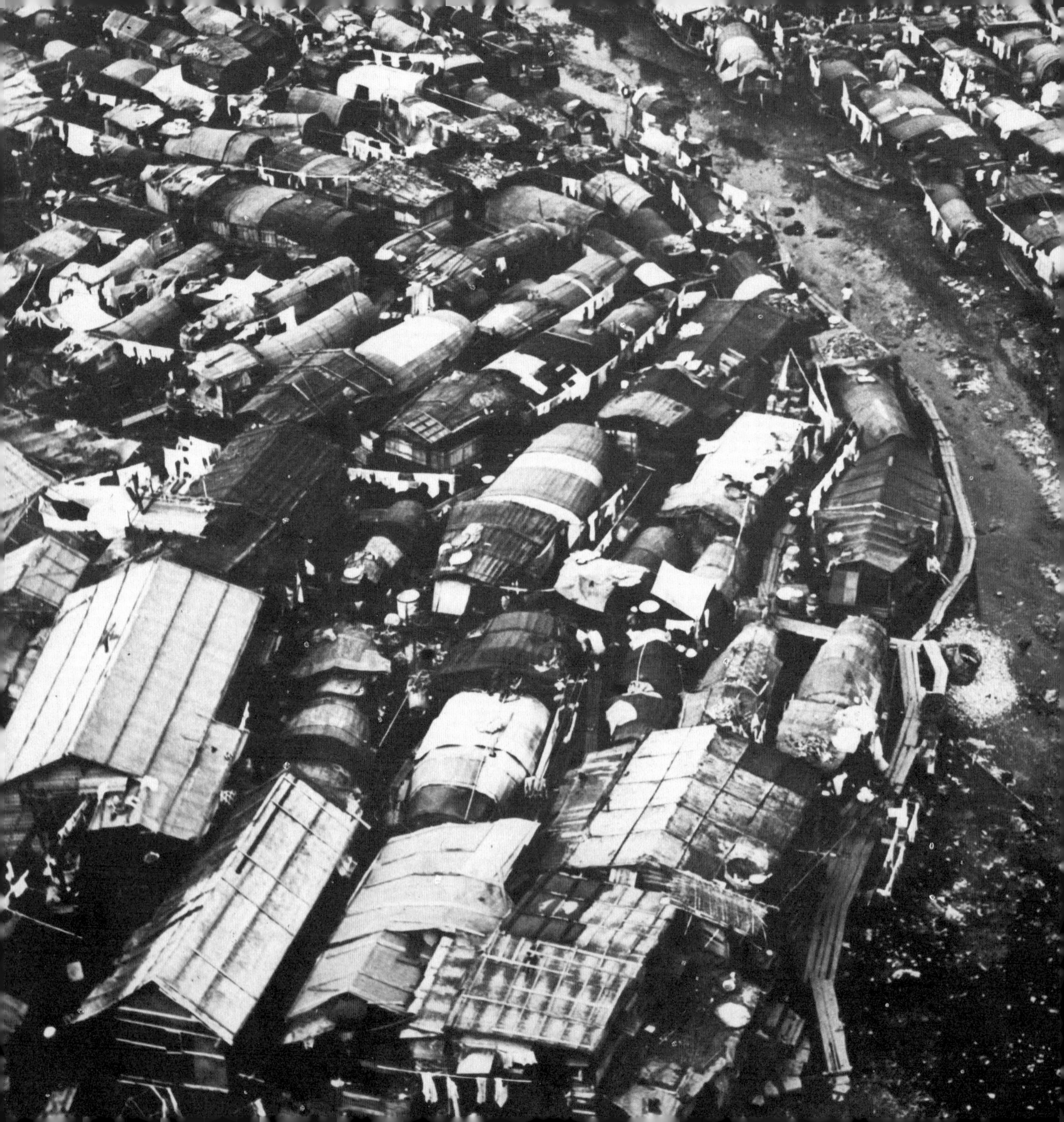

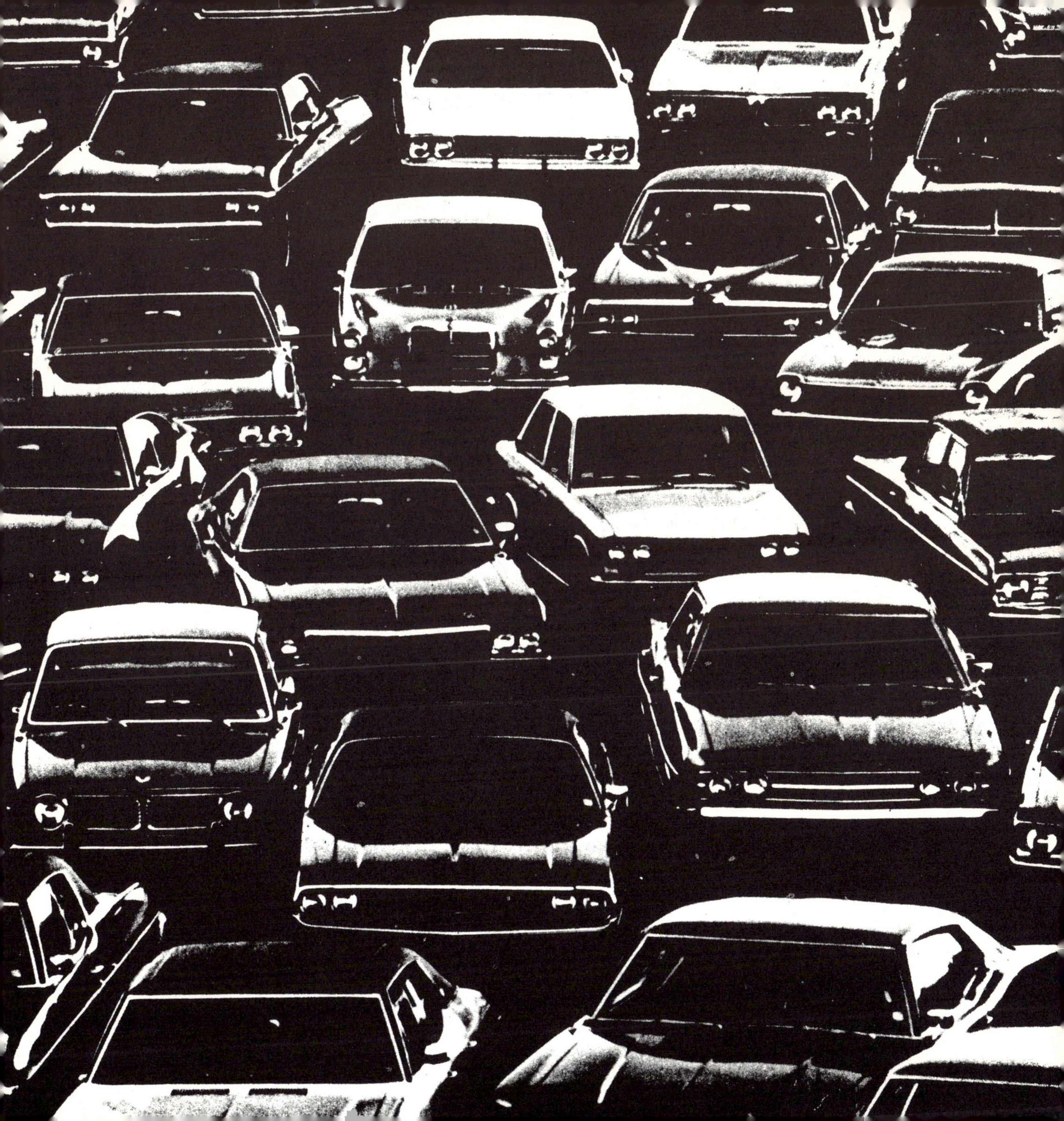

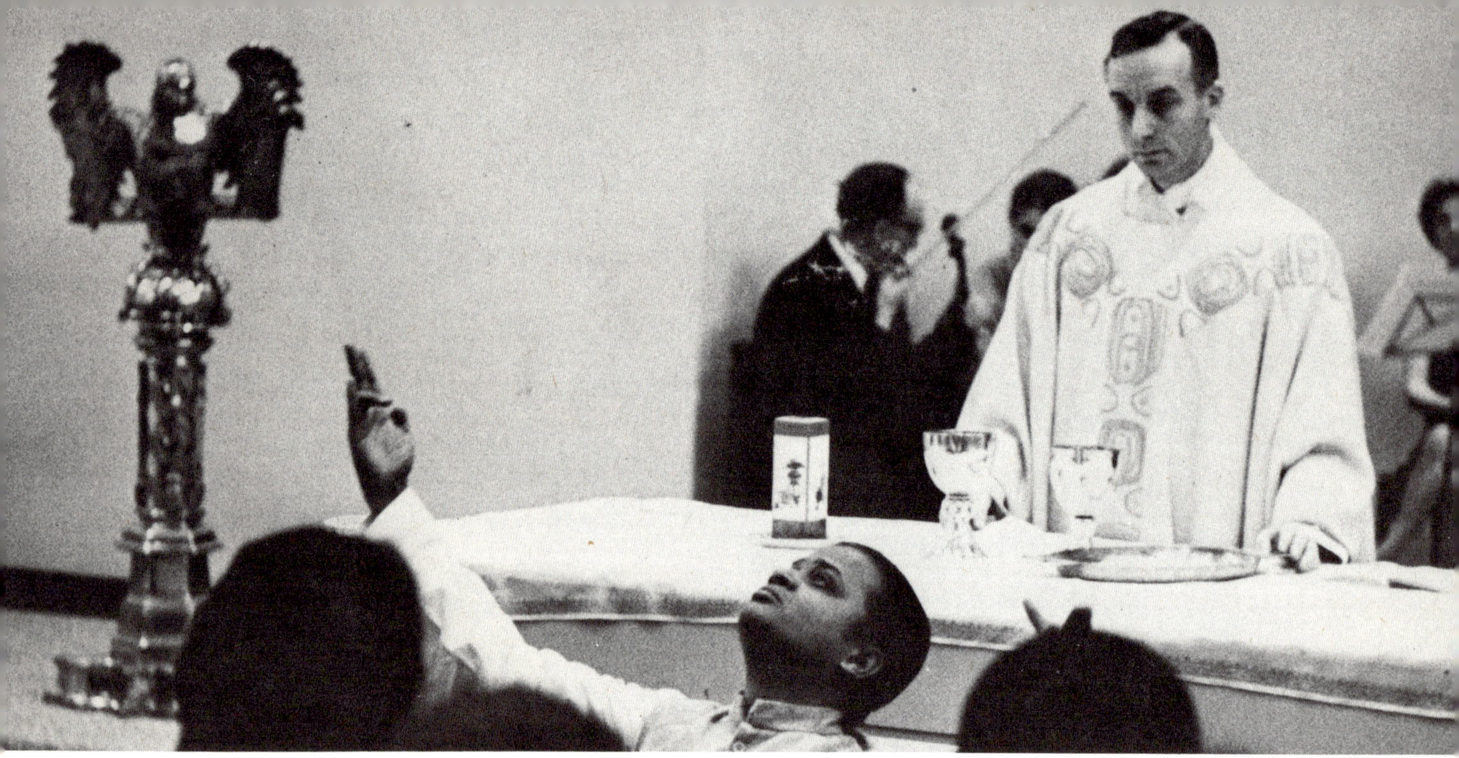
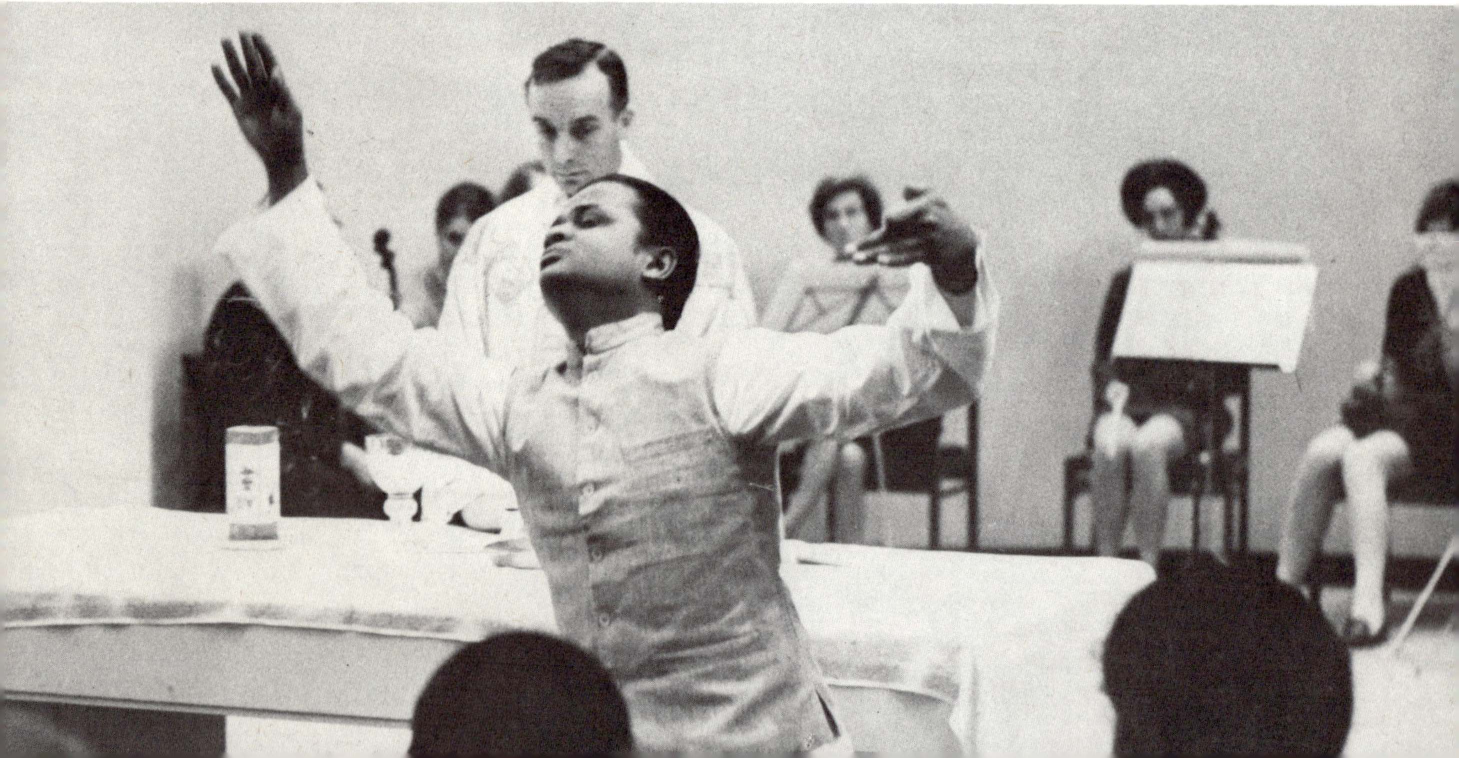

Fragments... miscellany

Logical coherence is an invention of the mind. It does not necessarily relate to celebration. A celebration may be a cluster of events, songs, dances, readings. Its sequences may be disjunctive, i.e., they may pop in and out of focus, or they may follow out a line of experience or an idea.

What follows in this short section are some fragments of celebration. They do not progress anywhere; they are as records of some experiences. They have been tasted.

Dancing the Lord's Prayer

Indian economist, Ronnie Sequiera, with Professor Rahner (photos left) in Munster at the College for Theology and Pastoral Work at Heerlen, Holland. He started training local people in Indian dances, while succeeding in evoking much creativity at an amazing rate.

The World Is Upside-Down

Music: I-to Loh
Text: Esther Rice

1. The world is up-side-down! The world is up-side-down! The false is true to peo-ple in this town. What can I do? What can I do?

2. The world is up-side-down! The world is up-side-down! They've lost the way — the ones who wear the crown. What can I say? What can I say?

3. The world is up-side-down! The world is up-side-down! "A lead-er be — a lead-er wins re-nown," they say to me, they say to me.

4. But life is still worthwhile,
   but life is still worthwhile
   if what I do
   can show for just a while
   that truth is true,
   that truth is true.

5. And life is still worthwhile,
   and life is still worthwhile
   if I but say,
   "To walk the second mile
   is the best way,
   is the best way."

6. My life will be worthwhile,
   my life will be worthwhile
   if, like a toy,
   I bring, with friendly smile,
   to one child, joy,
   to one child, joy.

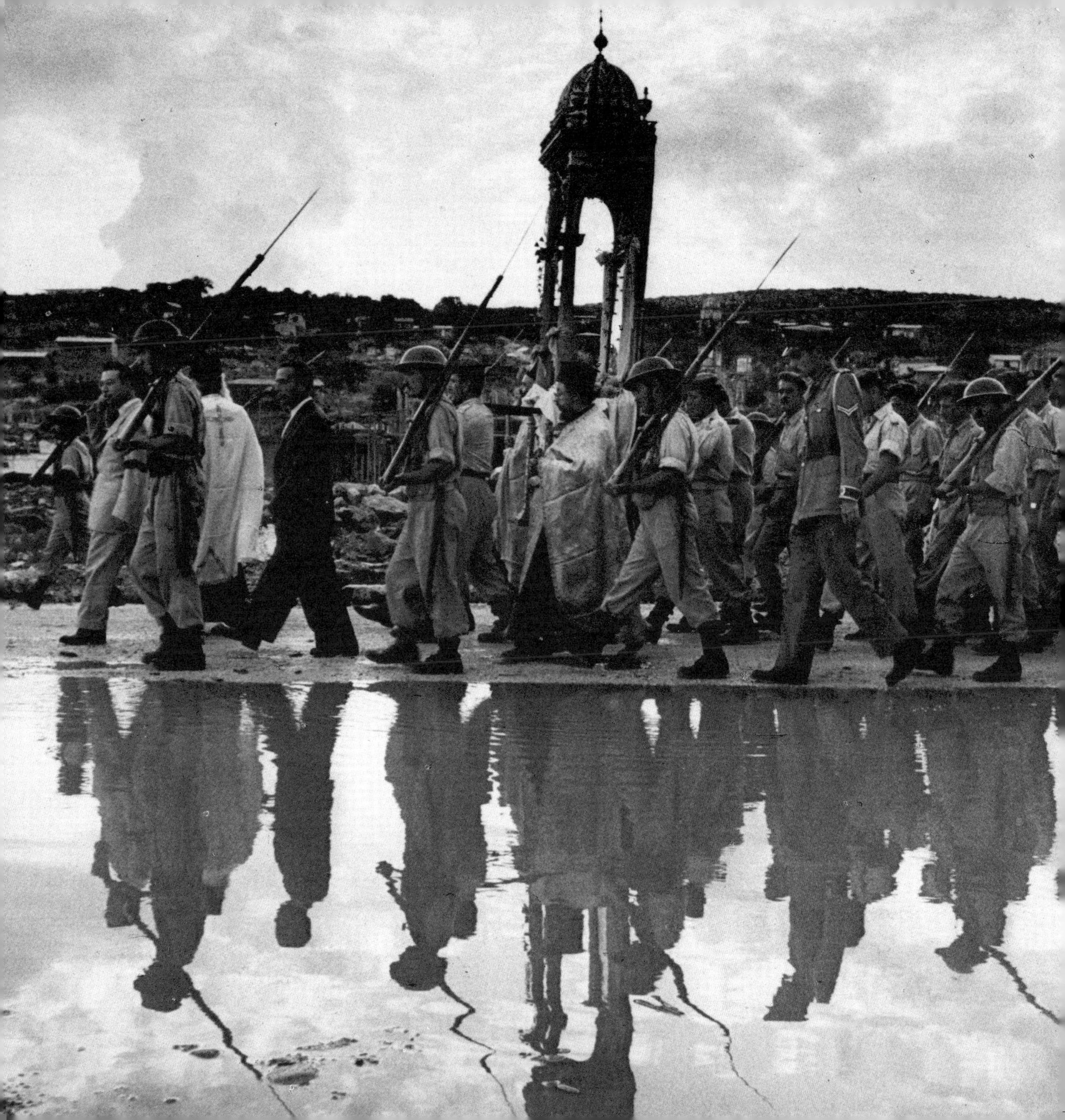

Four Events— Yushi at Bangkok

(Paragraph numbers correspond to photos going clockwise.)

1. Sometimes the unexpected dramatic provokes prayer, becomes worship, although the occasion or the circumstances may have quite a different intention.

At the Salvation Today Consultation, near Bangkok, early in 1973, a young Japanese poet-artist did some events, spontaneous and improvised. In a group working at *art and salvation* he had made a figure hung between two poles. It was much admired by others in the group who appreciated the immense work and skill that had gone into the making of the paper sculpture. Suddenly as the conversation lagged on a sleepy afternoon, he lit a match to his work before it was finished—not because he was unhappy with what he had done, but because he felt that the others were not seeing, not caring. . . . *The bombing of North Vietnam had recently resumed.*

2. At noontime, while the three hundred-odd delegates from all over the world were eating, Yushi staggered in, bull rushes tied about his body, carrying a rugged staff. . . . "Help me . . . h . . . e . . . l . . . p. . . ." An American started playing his synthesizer, sounds that reminded one of the description of the Holy Spirit at Pentecost. The beggar staggered out from the dining hall to the other side of an adjacent pool and spoke: "I baptize you with water; but he who is mightier than I is coming. . . . He will baptize you with the Holy Spirit and with

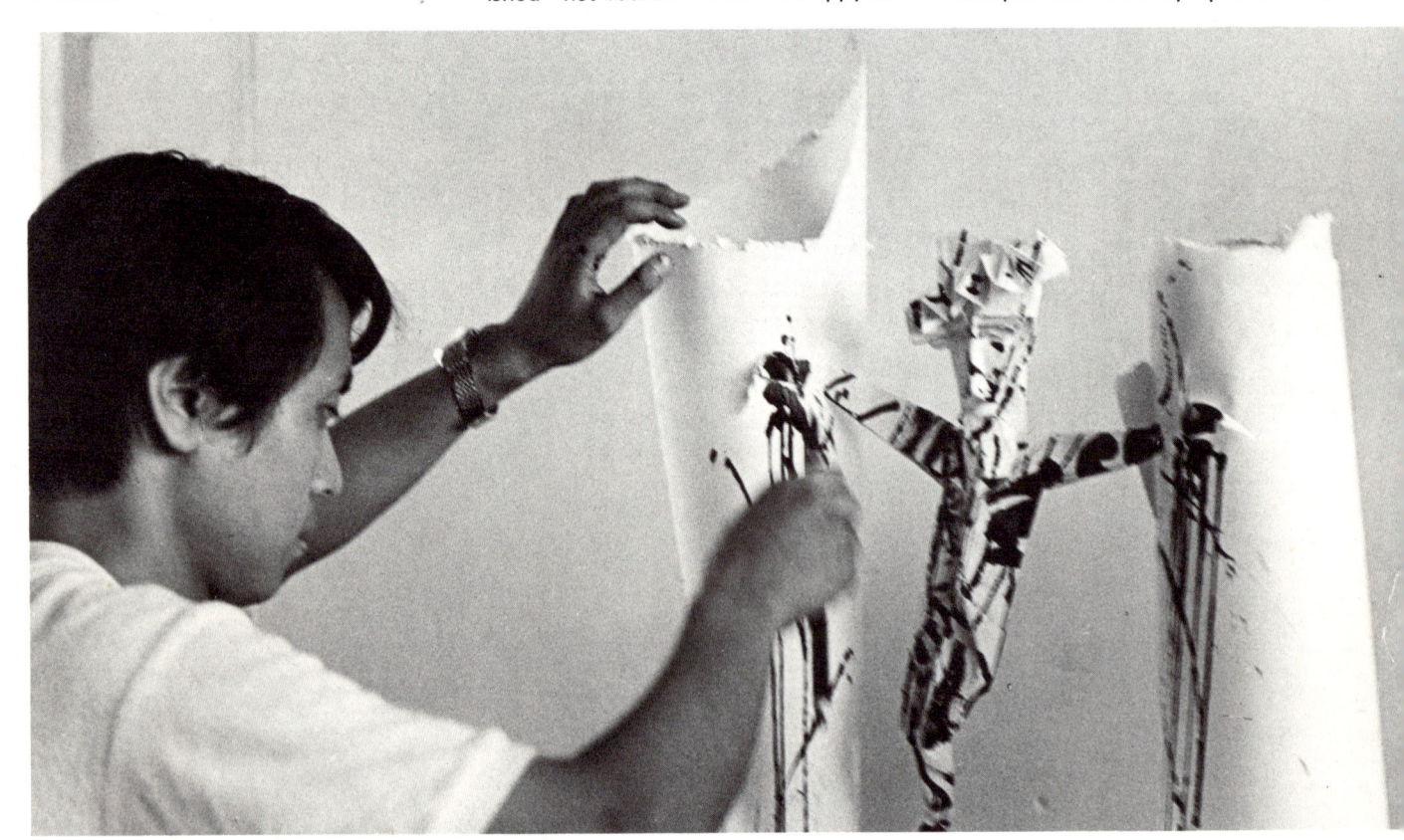

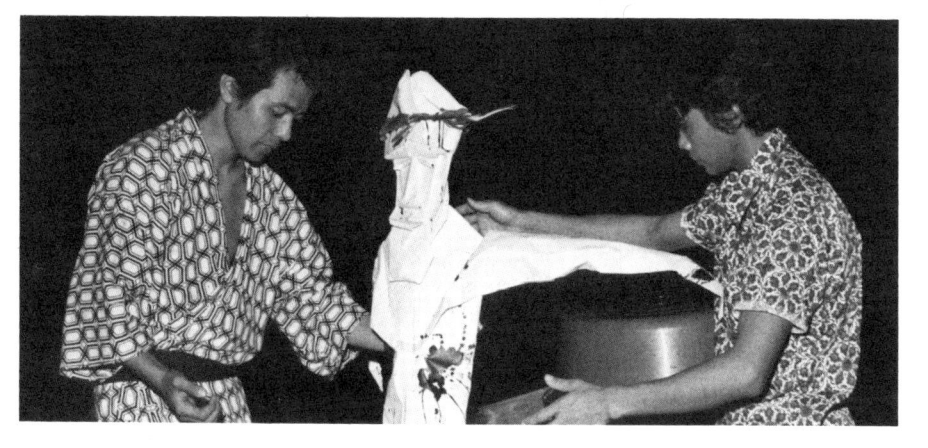

fire!" And he plunged into the water, finally to stagger out, exhausted! *Many diners were embarrassed... should they have responded?*

3. Again the dialogue wavered and lapsed. Suddenly Yushi staggered in, spread-eagled himself against the wall where pieces of art had been tacked... bloody, naked... dying. *Was that the way it was?... or is?*

4. The final worship service was one of unity: pieces of liturgy from Orthodox and Latin rites, singing from Africa and the West Indies, concluding with the "Salvation" song (see p. 21). And as the participants left, each encountered a crucifixion figure outside the entry. *It had not been there when they entered.*

Salvation in the Midst

During the Salvation Today Consultation near Bangkok, early in 1973, the participants from around the world decided, one evening, to *celebrate*. This is the outline of their celebration.

Was it worship? Some wondered. Others shouted Yes!

The participants were given a half sheet of paper with the following text. Nobody knew quite what would happen, but the musicians were there, and poets too . . . projectors and slides and films. . . .

And when it was done, just about everyone said "Marvelous!"

We offer you a chance to reflect by experience rather than by words. For the artist, what he or she does or tries to do is more real than words. Where there is freedom to face reality, to look, to see and to respond, is there not freedom from fear and so—signs of salvation?

We want to share with you some signs of the freedom to be and to let be so that we can join in the celebration of salvation. But we shall not explain nor shall we make statements in words. We hope that experience will call forth experience and that creativity, concentration and relaxation may be felt to be prayer, response and hope. If Christ is not 'named,' perhaps it is because he is the 'name above every name' who can be responded to in anything and in everything.

So:

(1) An opportunity to be quiet and to *look*—film and slides.
(2) Singing together and listening together.
(3) Many dimensions and in the midst.
(4) Dancing together.
(5) "Salvation" song.

Salvation

Words and Music by Roger Ortmayer and Ed Summerlin

Sal - va - tion, sal - va - tion.
1. A - tone, How 'bout it? In him no
2. Light, light
3. Vi - sion, Take a look
4. A - men, So be it, an
5. Truth, truth, Truth is not
6. In - her - it, No tax - es on in -
7. O - bey, O - bey the law of
8. Name, name, Je - sus Christ,

(1.) Can you win? A life to love? to___ be? He gives life, who - ly free!___
(2.) dark - ness is, No se - crets cov - ered up; He, too, ac - cept the cup.___
(3.) at your - self Al - so pain and pov - er - ty, No more let mis - 'ry be.___
(4.) ev - er - more, The true___ trust - ed one, Je - sus Christ, our God's Son.___
(5.) an - swer To make a bet - ter grade, Truth is love on pa - rade.___
(6.) her - i - tance; No one can take a - way, His love each bless - ed day.___
(7.) love; It's not as traf - fic rules, But fun to be love's fools.___
(8.) what a name! Shout it loud, and pro - claim Good News, his bless - ed name!___

Sal - va - tion names the game___ our hearts and lives to claim.___

claim.___ Sal - va - tion, sal - va - tion sal -

*"Salvation" is used for the first two measures each time, repeated ad lib.
**Each stanza has a different word for the "vamp" starting at measure 3 and is repeated ad lib.

© 1972 Summerlin Music.

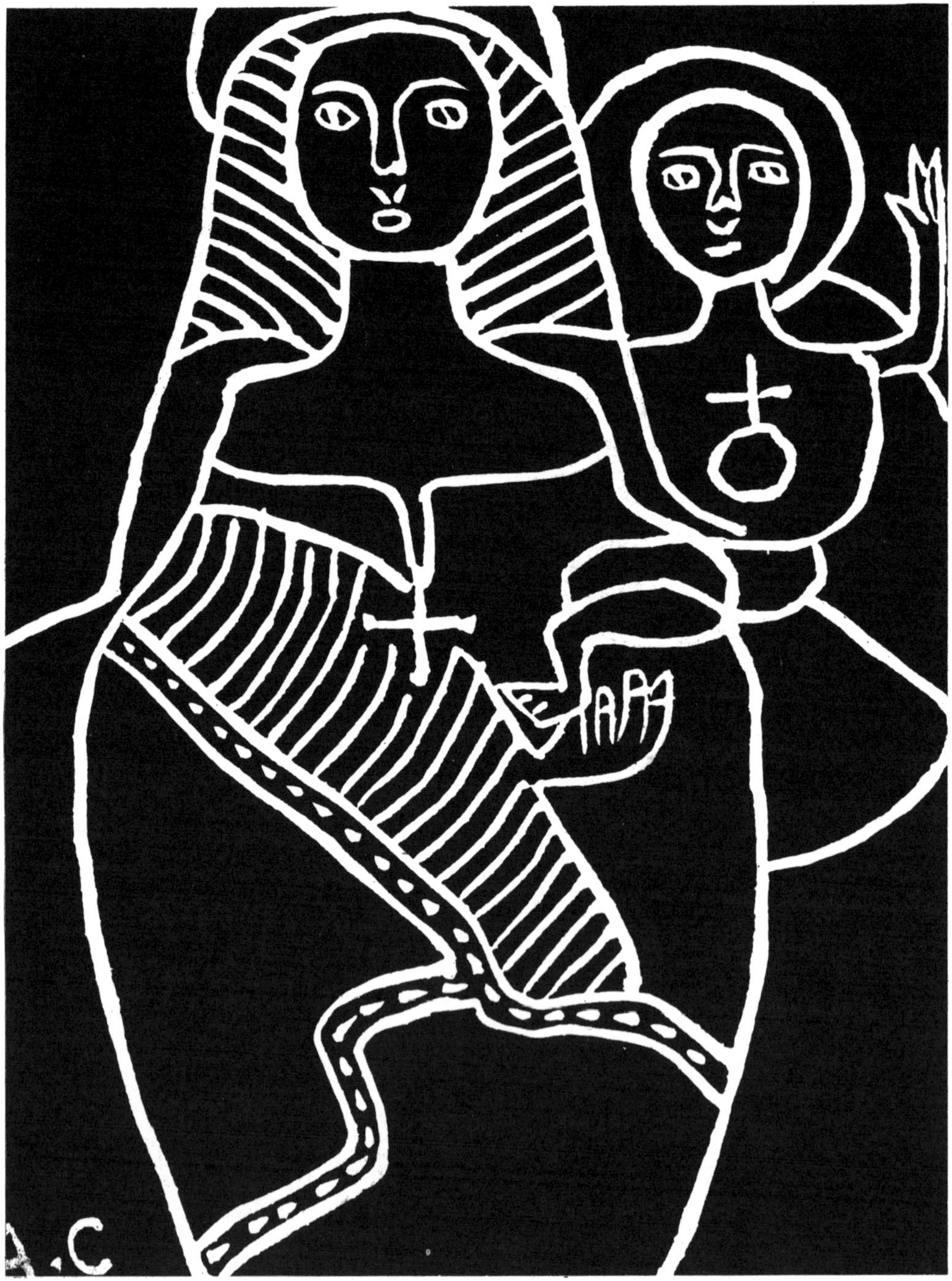
A.C

Christmas Message

By Azehim Anastasios Yannoulatos

from a Christmas service at the Ecumenical Center, Geneva, Switzerland.

... The universe was whispering to many thinkers: God is above us. A lot of thoughts of primitive religiosity were repeating: God is very far from us. The prophets in the Old Testament insisted that God is before you! But the incarnation of Christ brought the decisive message: God is with, within you. Christ assumed human nature in order to bring it to its first beauty and power and wholeness: to holiness. He did not come simply to reveal to mankind important truths, to offer principles and after to leave us; He came to transmit to humanity another quality of life: His divine life. To transform the human existence in its depth, to bring us to a condition which is yet a scandal for many: to the "theosis," to the participation in His own divine nature. He became man in order to make man God.

His incarnation constitutes a graft on the tree of mankind which continues to transform its sap, its identity and produce another kind of tree, a new humanity. The last day, the "eschata," the great day for which God laid the foundation of the universe has begun. The process is going on. We believe that we participate in its final accomplishment. In the Old Testament the ultimate goal of the eschatological period is the vision of God's glory (Isa. 66:18), but the New Testament reveals that the call of God is to something more: to be glorified with Him (Rom. 8:17). Our participation in this glory has already begun with our incorporation into Christ.

Although these are fundamental truths, a part of my heart is full of the temptation to cry: Oh, all these as such are words, cold words, for theological conferences, for unrealistic sermons. Words, cold words for books. How is it possible that all these symbols, the words, the ideas, the truths, be transformed to a personal reality? To a power for my weakness, to an answer for my deep existential agony, to hope and power and life? How is it possible to participate in the real life of Christ, to be in Him, to be a real personal symbol of His presence for this world? To participate truly in His great adventure, in His boldness to love a world which would not respond to his love?

I know that here is the crucial personal issue facing Christmas. But I cannot answer these questions. I try to be ecumenical: That is, to ask questions without answering. I escape. But I have, as always, a good reason for that: Time is over. I escape ... Excuse me. ...

Liturgies United in Prayer

"Doing" liturgy is the most distinctive act in the corporate life of Christians.

Theologizing is a second or third remove from what Christians do in worship. It is a reflection upon prayer life.

In the present situation, as liturgies suffer revision, necessarily, there is much that is new, yet in print it often seems to be the "same old stuff." Probably more important than the text, or outlines, of liturgies is their style. Giving the text of a service alone may be just "dry bones."

Most experimental liturgies are fugitive in nature—the experience is seldom recorded. Also, different cultures and peoples work at varying rhythms, and what may seem on paper to be familiar material might well have been an exciting development if experienced.

In spite of such drawbacks, however, it does seem worthwhile to record here some of the services done in recent years. The following come from a variety of geographical areas as well as cultural situations. The service which concludes a central European dialogue between Marxists, Freudians and Christians is a bit wordy (as Marx and Freud were!) and quite different in texture from that of medical students in Taiwan, or that of a lay group in Geneva, or that of a native African group.

The most profitable "use" of these liturgies does not seem to be attempting to follow them literally (though there may be some occasions to do so) but to taste, or use fragments. If you do choose to use a liturgy in its entirety, make its use more effective by changing references to people, masculine pronouns, current happenings or hymns to fit your situation.

Experimental Form of Worship

The early Christians not only celebrated the Eucharist, but the Eucharistic Meal was often enacted with the agape or love meal. The latter was the main expression of the reality of their unity in Christ and of the desire and commitment to deepen unity.

A new beginning—the need for sharing among ourselves (Acts 2: 42-47) and with others (Matthew 15: 34-46).

A Confession of Faith:

I believe in God, the Creator of all things and Maker of all men, yet who does not reign according to unchangeable laws, or will that inequalities and injustice should remain.

I believe in God, the Great Subversive Agent on behalf of the poor and needy, who sustains us to live for the Creation of a new society.

I believe in Jesus Christ, who shared and responded creatively to every part of our human experience and was crucified at an age when today he would have been too young for important work in the church.

I believe in Jesus Christ, who through his obedience to the Father, the intensity of his love for others and his resurrection after death, unites in one personality all those who obey his call.

I believe in the Holy Spirit, who gives men and women the strength to do what is just and right, and gives to the unending cosmic dimension every act of service and compassion.

I believe in the Holy Spirit, who helps us selfish individuals to transcend the barriers of ethnic, racial, cultural and linguis-

Prepared by the Aikya Group
U.T.C. Bangalore, India

tic differences, and unites us as a single fellowship.

Hymn: —"Christ is the Lord of All."

Preparation for the Breaking of Bread.

Confession:

I have fallen, Lord,
once more.
I can't go on, I'll never succeed.
I am ashamed, I don't dare look at you.
And yet I struggled, Lord, for I knew you were right near me, bending over me, watching.
But temptation blew like a hurricane
And instead of looking at you I turned my head away,
I stepped aside
While you stood, silent and sorrowful,
Like the spurned fiancé who sees his loved one carried off by his rival.

I'm so ashamed that I feel like crawling to avoid being seen,
I'm ashamed of being seen by my friend,
I'm ashamed of being seen by you, Lord,
For you loved me, and I forgot you.
I forgot you because I was thinking of myself,
And one can't think of several persons at once.
One must choose, and I chose.

Prayer—requests and intercessions (members of the congregation are invited to offer requests).

Breaking of Bread:

Leader (L): God alone is our peace.
Response (R): None but Jesus is our liberator.

L: We affirm the spirit of love.
R: We offer it to the world.
L: This is the bread of life.
R: Here is the cup of freedom.

A member of the congregation:
God is not dead
God is bread
The bread is rising
Bread means revolution
Revolution is love
Win with love
Jesus is winning
The world is coming to a beginning
The whole world is watching
Organize for a new world
Plant the peace garden
The liberated zone is at hand.

A member of the congregation will ask God to use us to accomplish his purpose.

L: Peace be with you.
R: And with you.
L: Lift up your hearts.
R: We lift them up to our liberator.
L: Let us give thanks to the power of creation.
R: It is right for us to do so.

A member of the congregation will offer a prayer of adoration.

All: Holy, Holy, Holy is the power beyond all powers,
The fullness of the whole world is his glory
Blessed is the one who comes in his name;

L: Truly holy, truly blessed is our heavenly Father. Because of your love, you gave your only Son Jesus Christ unto us. Thank you Lord Jesus, for though you were in the form of God, you emptied yourself and took the form of a servant and were born into this world. You gave yourself for us on the Cross to redeem the world. Today we recall how at your last freedom meal with your friends you took the loaf as we do, said thanks over it and broke it, and gave it to them, saying: "Take, eat; this is my body broken for you: Do this in remembrance of me." Also after the meal you took the cup, said thanks, and gave it to them saying: "Drink this, all of you; for this cup is the unending constitution of a new society in my blood, poured out for liberation from your guilt. Do this, whenever you drink it, in remembrance of me."

R: Your death we recall,
Your resurrection we announce,
Your second coming we await.
Glory be to you O Lord.

L: That constitution is his new way of sacrificial reconciliation of which this meal is our permanent reminder. He put himself so completely in others that nothing of him could die. Therefore in the liberated zone of his spirit we are made whole and given new life.

R: So may it be, here and everywhere,
Now and always — Come, Lord Jesus.

L: We who are many are one body,
For we share the one loaf.

All take Communion.

Lord's Prayer.

Look at all my trials and tribulations
Thinking in a gentle pool of wine,

African Service

Order of Service

Prelude:
Missa Luba with drums, from the Congo

Call To Worship: (all standing)

Leader: O, come, let us sing unto the Lord, Let us rejoice in the strength of his Salvation. Let us come before his presence with Thanksgiving and show ourselves glad in him with psalms.

Hymn: "Thine is the Glory"

Responsive Reading: Micah 4:1-4

Leader: It shall come to pass in the latter days that the mountain of the house of the Lord shall be established as the highest of the mountains, and shall be raised up above the hills;

All: and peoples shall flow to it,

Leader: and many nations shall come, and say:

All: "Come, let us go up to the mountain of the Lord, to the house of the God of Jacob; that he may teach us his ways and we may walk in his paths."

Leader: For out of Zion shall go forth the law, and the word of the Lord from Jerusalem.

All: He shall judge between many peoples, and shall decide for strong nations afar off;

Leader: and they shall beat their swords into plowshares, and their spears into pruning hooks;

All: nation shall not lift up sword against nation, neither shall they learn war any more;

Leader: but they shall sit every man

What's that in the bread, it's gone to my head,
From this evening until morning life is fine
Always hoped that I'd be an apostle
Knew that I would make it if I tried
Never thought that love could solve so many problems,
Till we stood as one together by his side.

Look at all my trials and tribulations
Sinking in a gentle pool of wine
Don't disturb me now I can see the answers,
From this evening until morning life is fine
Always hoped I'd be an apostle
Knew that I would make it if I tried
Never thought that love could solve so many problems,
Till we stood as one together by his side.

The Peace.

Prayer of Thanksgiving and Grace.

CHRIST IS THE LORD OF ALL

Christ is the Lord of the smallest atom,
Christ is the Lord of outer space,
Christ is the Lord of the constellations,
Christ is the Lord of everyplace:
    Of the farthest star, Of the coffee bar,
    Of the length of the Berlin Wall;
    Of the village green, Of the Asian scene:
CHRIST IS THE LORD OF ALL.

Christ is the Lord of the human heartbeat,
Christ is the Lord of every breath;
Christ is the Lord of man's existence,
Christ is the Lord of life and death:
    In the city store, By the surfing shore,
    On the sword with the bat and ball;
    Where the people flee, Of the refugee,
CHRIST IS THE LORD OF ALL.

Christ is the Lord of our thoughts and feelings,
Christ is the Lord of all we plan;
Christ is the Lord of man's decision,
Christ is the Lord of total man:
    In the local street, where the people meet,
    In the church of the nearby hall;
    In the factory, In the family
CHRIST IS THE LORD OF ALL.

Christ is the Lord of our love and courtship,
Christ is the Lord of man and wife;
Christ is the Lord of the things we care for
CHRIST IS THE LORD OF ALL OUR LIFE.

Reprinted from *THE GUARDIAN*, Dec. 22, '71.

under his vine and under his fig tree, and none shall make them afraid;

All: for the mouth of the Lord of hosts has spoken.

Leader: Glory be to the Father and to the Son and to the Holy Spirit,

All: As it was in the beginning is now and ever shall be world without end.

Amen.

Prayer: by African prophet Ntsikana. The prayer is in the form of music. His clear voice ringing down the valley, summoning his people, gave rise to the name Ntsikana's Bell.

Translation from Xhosa:
Thou art the great God—he who is in heaven.
Thou art the Creator of life, thou makest the regions above.
Thou art the hunter who hunts for souls.
Thou art the great Mantle which covers us.
Thou art he whose hands are with wounds.
Thou art he whose feet are with wounds.
Thou art he whose blood is a trickling stream.
Thou art he whose blood was spilled for us.

Scripture Readings: Acts 17: 22-31, Romans 2: 12-29

Hymn: (in Bemba from Zambia, see pg.47)

Meditation: Poetry (see "A Handful of Prayers," p. 51).

Prayers of Intercession:

Leader: Lord, I bring before you the needs of all the people of this continent and I pray that your will may be done in and by them. . . .

Response: Thy will be done on earth as it is in heaven

Leader: Its rulers and all its government officials

Response: Thy will be done on earth as it is in heaven

Leader: The ministers and congregations of Christian bodies

Response: Thy will be done on earth as it is in heaven

Leader: Judges, magistrates, counsel and all engaged in courts of law. . . .

Response: Thy will be done on earth as it is in heaven

Leader: All prisoners, and all who are suffering for conscience' sake

Response: Thy will be done on earth as it is in heaven

Leader: Broken and unhappy homes, and families divided by law or by economic circumstances . . . .

Response: Thy will be done on earth as it is in heaven

Leader: The poor, the hungry, the badly housed, the underpaid, all who suffer from injustice. Those who are afraid. . . .

Response: Thy will be done on earth as it is in heaven

Leader: Those who have become bitter and hopeless. Those who hate and do not want to love. Those who condone injustice by silence. . . .

Response: Thy will be done on earth as it is in heaven

Leader: Those who are blind to the needs of others. . . .

Response: Thy will be done on earth as it is in heaven

Leader: Those who in any way are witnessing to the truth; those who by their works are succouring the afflicted; those who are working to promote a spirit of brotherhood amongst the races of this continent. . . .

Response: Thy will be done on earth as it is in heaven

Leader: My own sins, blindness, prejudices, stubbornness, stupidity. . . .

Response: Thy will be done on earth as it is in heaven

Leader: Light to know what is your will and courage to do it. . . .

Response: Thy will be done on earth as it is in heaven

Leader: Your glory, O God, your justice, your love, your peace, your will. . . .

Response: Thy will be done on earth as it is in heaven

Leader: O God, the Father of all mankind, we beseech Thee so to inspire the people of this land with the spirit of justice, truth and love, that in all our dealings one with another we may show forth our brotherhood in Thee; for the sake of Jesus Christ our Lord.

African Anthem by choir: Nkosi Sikelela Iafrika (or see p. 63)

Benediction and Dismissal

Freedom songs played while congregation goes out.

An Ecumenical Act of Thanks

This ecumenical liturgy was developed in Argentina in October 1967. A flood had destroyed many homes in the region, and Catholic and Protestant groups joined together in relief work. The ecumenical service developed from the joint work, and was attended by many people in the area.

I. Praise

a. Reading from Psalm 32

b. Song

II. Intercession

a. Thematic Reading

— for the children, the elderly and all those who are still sleeping on the ground and on mattresses, with neither pillows nor blankets

— for the families who live in poor neighborhoods without medical attention, and without sufficient help from public officials

— for those who fear tomorrow, because they are without anything, those who are alone, and who have no steady work

— so that among them, neighboring families will help selflessly, that the ghettos may unite and work together without enclosing themselves in selfish interests, and so that relations between the government and the peoples will be relations of understanding, respect and mutual collaboration.

b. Lord, together we pray for our brothers who continue to suffer because of the flood, both for their physical suffering and the indignities to which they are exposed. Give them what they need to survive; and to us and all those with decision-making power, give us the spirit to continue struggling with them, so that in this region and everywhere in the world everyone may live and develop with the dignity that you, Lord, want for your children. AMEN.

III. Proclamation of the Word

a. Reading from biblical text

b. Message

IV. Act of Thanks

a. Singing or reading of Psalm 23

b. Litany

— For Your Son, Jesus Christ, Savior and Guide of your people
— WE THANK YOU LORD

— For the love of Jesus Christ, who makes us one Church
— WE THANK YOU LORD

— Because you inspire us to serve our fellowman
— WE THANK YOU LORD

— Because you show us your work in every man, woman and child
— WE THANK YOU LORD

— Because you make us understand that our life was given to us that we may live it for others
— WE THANK YOU LORD

V. Benediction

Minister — Blessings to the Lord

People — We give thanks to God

Minister — May the peace of God, Father, Son and Holy Ghost be with you and yours for now and for evermore. AMEN

Thank You Lord

**A Song poem
by Homero Perera**

I.

For sweating along with them
as they take from the earth
the fruit which makes them slaves,
Thank You, Lord.

For crying together with them
when the harvest finally ends
and they reap bitterness,
Thank You, Lord.

(Refrain)

Lord, thank you Lord
Lord, I give you thanks
We will never understand
how much love you brought
to share in
our suffering.

II.

For suffering hunger with them
when the little they earn
is spent on paying bills,
Thank You, Lord.

For suffering cold with them
under a roof of leaves and branches,
Thank You, Lord.

(Refrain)

III.

For being in the middle of them
when they were beaten
for asking for higher wages,
Thank You, Lord.

For also being with them
when they returned home
with two empty hands,
Thank You, Lord.

(Refrain)

United Service

(as used by Roman Catholic and Protestant Christians together in Taiwan)

(Acts 1-5 are dramatic presentations and interpretations of the individual passages.)

I. Act 1 *Adam and Eve* (The Fall), Genesis 3:1-24

Litany

Leader: We have misused our free will and have disobeyed the will of God.

People: O Gracious Lord, forgive us.

Leader: We have tried to hold on to a moment's pleasure and have let slip the blessings which are eternal.

People: O Gracious Lord, forgive us.

Leader: We have been unwilling to accept our own responsibilities and have blamed our sins on other people instead of having the courage to confess that we have done wrong.

People: O Gracious Lord, forgive us.

II. Act 2 *Noah*, Genesis 6: 5-22, 7:1-5, 17-24, 8:15-22

Litany

Leader: We belong to a violent world exposed to pounding waves and raging winds; we seek blindly for peace and happiness.

People: O God of righteousness, save and deliver us.

Leader: Our surroundings are full of wickedness and evil; we have fallen into the pit which we ourselves dug and we cannot escape.

People: O God of righteousness, save and deliver us.

Leader: Give us hearts burning with zeal for true righteousness, earnestly striving to transform what is bad even at the cost of our lives.

People: O God of righteousness, save and deliver us.

III. Act 3 *Abraham and Isaac*, Genesis 22:1-19

Litany

Leader: Lord, we constantly misinterpret and suspect your purpose and your will, and so we do not know what to do.

People: O God of promises, teach us how to submit.

Leader: We cannot grasp your promises; we half believe and half doubt; we have no strength to fulfill your command.

People: O God of promises, teach us how to submit.

Leader: You ask us to offer our love, will, concerns, talent, and treasure as living sacrifices.

People: O God of promises, teach us how to submit.

IV. Act 4 *Jesus' Death and Resurrection*, I Corinthians 15:1-28

Litany

Leader: Jesus Christ by his self-sacrifice has saved us and all men.

People: Almighty God, we thank and praise you.

Leader: By the victory of the Cross, the hope of peace and eternal life has been given to mankind.

People: Almighty God, we thank and praise you.

Leader: The holy church throughout the world unitedly witnesses that Christ, the light of the world, is the way to eternal life.

People: Almighty God, we thank and praise you.

V. Act 5 *One Church*, Ephesians 4:1-16 (Or I Corinthians 12:12-13)

VI. Prayer for Unity

VII. Hymn: "In Christ There Is No East or West"

Sunday Worship

(originally used at the Kaohsiung Medical College Student Center at Kaohsiung, Taiwan)

1. Prelude (silent prayer)

2. Call to Worship:

Leader: Lord, we are trying to find ourselves here in order to find the meaning and purpose of life for our time and situation.

People: Lord, we are trying to find ourselves here in order to know you more deeply.

3. Prayer of Dedication

Leader: Colossians 3:12-14

People: I Corinthians 13:13

4. Praise: Hymn

5. Prayer

Leader: O God, we ask you to pour out your Holy Spirit on us. Help us serve you more cheerfully so we can serve our fellows and all mankind.

People: Cast out everything which breaks and hinders the growing bonds of love between us—hate, pride, resentment, selfishness, greed and prejudice.

All: Give us the determination to make progress so that all our lives we may seek after your holy and perfect will. In Jesus' name. Amen.

6. Reading: Matthew 25:31-46

7. Prayer: Father, help us at whatever cost to give the best to our neighbor, through our love to help others to find Christ. O God, support us with your strength so that in our daily lives we may fight against all oppression, unrighteousness and selfishness in mankind. May we increasingly manifest your truth, your righteousness and your peaceful purpose on earth as in heaven. In Jesus' name. Amen.

8. Praise: "They'll Know We Are Christians By Our Love"

9. Sermon

10. Prayer

Leader:
a. If we had a lecture which would move men and could rely on every method of spreading it over the whole globe. . . .
b. If we could go down to the depths of the sea and set foot on the moon and the planets. . . .
c. If we could carry out a heart transplant, and develop tremendously powerful drugs. . . .
d. If we could rely on a computer to solve all our questions and uncover all mysteries. . . .

People: If we could do all these things . . . but had no love, we would count for nothing.

Leader:
a. If the hungry are never fed. . . .
b. If the naked are never clothed. . . .
c. If the sick have no one to look after them. . . .
d. If the old are rejected and the young die an early death. . . .

People: If we ourselves had all knowledge and skill and ability . . . but had no love, then it would all be valueless, in fact it would be a curse.

Leader: Lord, teach us where the lovely people are.

People: Help us to relate to them with warmth and sincerity.

Leader: Lord, teach us where the isolated people and outsiders are.

People: Help us to live in harmony with them.

11. Lord's Prayer

12. Offering (for an orphanage)

13. Notices

14. Hymn

15. Benediction

16. Silent Prayer

A Liturgy For Pentecost

The text is in two columns—column one the actual responsive service, column two commentary which may be incorporated in the responsive sections or may be used as a commentary to be read silently by participants.

I. The Preparation

(Assemble in hall, coffee)
(3 minute warning bell)

(Present at door, shaking hands)

(Offertory baskets at entrance to church)

(Joyful organ music—rising in crescendo at end)

(Priest enters, stands at back. All stand)

Priest:
I was glad when they said unto me, "Let us go into the house of the Lord."

All:
Our feet have been standing within thy gates, O Jerusalem.

Priest:
For the sake of my brothers and companions, I will say, "Peace be within you."

All:
For the sake of the household of the Lord our God we will seek your good.

Priest: (still at back)
Friends, we are met tonight once again because a man called Jesus died and then rose from the dead nearly 2000 years ago in Palestine. In this feast we shall be giving expression to our faith that Jesus Christ is the Lord, the Savior of the world. We shall be offering our praise, our thanksgiving and our prayers to his Father through him. And in the way he appointed, by our sharing in his body and his blood, he will again bind us to himself, and by his Spirit—the gift of whom we today particularly celebrate—enliven us for his service. So let us kneel in silence and remember who he was, an Holy Spirit of God come into our hearts, and unite us into the fellowship of thy church. Show us the way to truth and help us into greater confidence in thee. Above all, help us to remove self from our lives and to draw closer to Jesus Christ that he may be in us and we in him.

Amen.

(Organ starts immediately)

All stand

All:
Hymn: "Alleluia, Sing to Jesus"

II. The Word

(At end, Priest comes forward, goes behind table, picks up Bible and hands it to the reader who will come to the table—and then to the lectern. All sit)

Reader 1.
Our reading from the Old Testament comes from the prophecies of Joel, beginning at chapter 2, verse 28.

(Reader 1 returns to the table and gives Bible back to the Priest, who then hands it to Reader 2. Reader to the lectern)

Reader 2.
Our readings from the Apostles' letters to the churches comes from Paul's first to the Corinthians, beginning at chapter 12, verse 4.

Commentary:

It is the community which celebrates. We must meet and know one another, conscious also that we are there in the name of the whole church and of the whole world.

We accept him as our man (before, not after).

We put aside our money to be offered later.

Nothing dim or timid—it is a celebration.

From a Psalm (122) of pilgrimage to Jerusalem.

Peace equals salvation, the wholeness of blessing and fulfillment.

We recall, in very bare, elementary terms why we are here. We can fill this out for ourselves in the silence.

(Prepared by the Lay Group of Holy Trinity, Geneva.)

Invocation to the unseen Spirit. Whatever is true, genuine and effective in this service will be His doing not ours.

We move to consider in more detail today's chosen aspects of the total biblical record.

The prophet, preaching probably soon after the return out of exile to Jerusalem, looks forward to the imminent day of the Lord, fearful and dangerous but rich with promise—since God's Spirit, formerly available only to special prophets, will be on all men. We remember how Peter used this as the text of his first Christian sermon. (Acts 2 14ff.).

Paul is stressing that, by baptism into Christ, we have all received the gifts of the Spirit, however different the particular functions these lead to.

(Reader 2 returns the Bible. Reader 3 remains in front of the table)
Priest:
(All stand)
Let us stand to hear the good news of Christ.

Reader 3.
Our reading from the Gospels comes from John, beginning at chapter 14, verse 15 and then in chapter 20, verse 19.

(Reader 3 returns Bible to Priest who, still holding it says. . . .)
Priest:
Lord Christ, consecrate us in truth.

All:
Thy word is Truth.

(Priest comes round in front of table)
Priest:
Please sit.

(All sit)

To help us realize more fully the meaning of what we have just heard, of the Spirit whose coming we celebrate and of this feast which under him we can enjoy, I'm going to read a sermon which John Chryscstom preached toward the end of the Fourth century, on Pentecost. It is called "The Gifts of the Holy Ghost."

(At end, Priest returns behind table and sits while all remain silent. After 3 minutes—)
Priest:
Sure of Christ's promised Spirit, available to us and to all men, we confess to our

---

Jesus at supper with the twelve on the last night is trying to prepare them for his death and what will happen after it. And then we read of it all beginning to come about—the story that has led to our being here.

We echo Jesus' final prayer for his disciples. (Jn. 17:17)

The address is for our understanding and meditation. It does not have to be new. The use of one preached by one of the greatest preachers in church history can help us to realize the tradition in which we are taking part.

faith in common with his people of every age and place.

(All stand)
I believe in one God, the Father Almighty ... (Nicene Creed)

(Organ starts)
All:
Hymn: "Come Down O Love Divine."

III. The Sacrament
1. The Offering
(At end of hymn all remain standing while the offering—bread, wine, water and money—is brought by a family. Priest comes forward to behind table and receives it)
All:

Take, Lord, into your possession, all my independence, my intelligence, my understanding and my entire will, all that I have, all that I own, is your gift to me and I now return it to you, to be used according to your will. Give me only your love and your grace, it is all I need.

(Priest comes round in front of the table. The family return to their places)
Priest:

Today we rejoice in the fact that on that day of Pentecost the disciples were given the conviction that Jesus was Lord and that his Spirit had come upon them; for their witness that same promise of the Spirit's presence is offered to us in turn today. Jesus rules over all and by his Spirit we can enter into his rule, can see meaning and purpose in all things; he is not conquered by failure or inadequacy in men, but by his Spirit is always ready to forgive and to lead us further; Jesus is the fullness of man; his Spirit inspires us with his concern for healing and wholeness; his healing power can work also through us. Jesus is love; his Spirit infects us with his love and solidarity with all men, nerves us to respond to the opportunities of this new life and overthrows all our selfish desires for success and security.

So let us hold ourselves and all men into his sure promises:

(All sit or kneel. Leader stands at back of church)
Leader I.

So much has come true, so much has failed to come true; Lord, accept our thanksgiving and our repentance.

Leader I:

Your rule; all princes and parties which set themselves up as supreme have crumbled and will crumble.

You are bringing our nations into unity and leading men to discover the ways of health and wealth. Yet we have had little vision of your great purposes; our nations care much more to win out in the competition for gain and power than for the welfare of all; and we have preferred to follow the selfish aims of a successful career and comfortable living.
Lord, give us eyes to see, and the courage to make a new start.
All:
We forgive one another; may we know your forgiveness.
(silence)

In the offertory we make not just a part, but the whole of our selves available to Christ, by a prayer of Ignatius Loyola.

In this promise we remind ourselves of the great themes of the sermon...

and of their relevance to our prayers and thanksgiving.

The things we give thanks for will always also be occasion for regret and repentance. We need not worry about our feelings in prayer being muddled. Life is never unambiguous and what matters is that it is our life and the life of the world that is held before God. In the silences we can apply the prayers to ourselves and the circles in which we are involved.

Leader I:
You are our humanity; now we know that all races of men are basically equal in promise, that it is in the power of man to change both nature and his own society, that we are not limited by any impersonal force outside ourselves. If we would let each other, we are free to grow into You and to bring all creation with us. Yet we still squabble and mistrust one another; we have clung to what we know and like when faced with new situations. Even in the church we will not risk what we have for what we might become.
Lord, give us eyes to see and the courage to make a new start.
All:
We forgive one another; may we know your forgiveness.
(silence)

Leader I:
You are love; and are teaching us at least to see the needs of our fellow men, at least to ensure that our minimum requirements are met, and to accept help from one another. Our welfare states could at last become a welfare world. Yet we let the gap between rich and poor grow wider, we take little notice of those who warn, and give little support to those who are working on the intricate technical problems of universal neighbor-love. Even in the church we close our eyes to the great questions and settle down to enjoy our immediate relationships.
Lord, give us eyes to see and the courage to make a new start.
All:
We forgive one another; may we know your forgiveness.
(silence)

Priest:
On your Cross, Lord, you silently triumphed over a world that has remained rebellious. Grant us in the silence of this sacrament to suffer with You and know your victory.
Leader II (also at back):
Let us begin our new start by holding the life of the world and our lives in this city in intercession before the Father.
We think of those who rule, the governments of our countries and their representatives here; the WHO and all its political undertakings, the disarmament conference, the conference on trade and development, the Kennedy round; the rulers of this city, the judges and the police; the leaders of our churches and those who meet in the World Council of Churches; all bosses in offices and parents in families.
Lord, you can set us on the right path and bring us to the right end.
All:
And may our Spirit guide our minds and hands.
(silence)

Leader II:
We think of all who are working for a fuller and richer life. Scientists at CARE and

medical researchers in the hospitals uncovering new secrets of power and life; all involved in the WHO, the telecommunications Union and the Technical Assistance Board; all those in the banks and the commercial firms of this city; those inventing and distributing new products; all teachers in schools and colleges; all organizers of leisure time activities, the YMCA and the YWCA.
Lord, You can set us on the right path and bring us to the right end.

All:
And may your Spirit guide our minds and hands.

(silence)

Leader II:
We think of all who foster or need human love; our families, our children; all who at this time are thinking about love and marriage; those who are sick or bereaved; all working in the Red Cross and the High Commission for Refugees; those beside us in this church and those involved in the fellowship or other churches; those responsible for spreading news through press or broadcasting; and ourselves—that the demands of love may be our constant and dominant criteria;
Lord, You can set us on the right path and bring us to the right end.

All:
And may your Spirit guide our minds and hands.

(silence)

(Priest, behind table)

2. Thanksgiving

(All stand. The two deacons come and stand on either side of the Priest.)

Priest:
Lift up your hearts.

All:
We lift them up unto the Lord.

Priest:
Let us give thanks to our Lord God.

All:
It is fitting and right so to do.

Priest:
It is indeed fitting and right, and our most joyful duty, that we should at all times and in all places give thanks to thee, O Lord, Holy Father, Almighty and Everlasting God; through Jesus Christ our Lord, by whose promise the Spirit came down from heaven upon the Apostles that day, in a sound of thunder and a mighty wind, to teach them and to lead them into all truth, giving them the gift of many languages and also new courage and energy to take the Gospel into all nations; by whom we too have been brought out of ignorance into knowledge and love of thee and given new energy to share in the service of thy son Jesus Christ. Therefore with all the saints in Heaven and earth we praise and magnify Thy glorious Name, evermore praising Thee and saying:

All:
Holy, holy, holy, Lord God of Hosts, Heaven and earth are full of Thy glory. Glory be to Thee, O Lord Most High. Amen.

Priest:
(breaks bread into two pieces at the appropriate moment) Almighty God, our Heavenly Father . . . (See I Corinthians 11:23-29) . . . who, in the same night as he was betrayed, which was the time of the Passover, took bread . . . drink it, in remembrance of Me. Therefore, O Father, we recall the blessed passion and death of Thy beloved Son, His mighty resurrection and glorious ascension until He comes again; and we here beseech Thee to send Thy Holy Spirit upon us and upon these gifts of bread and wine, that they may be the bread of eternal life and the cup of everlasting salvation. (See biblical reference for complete text.)

All:
Our Father . . . (Lord's Prayer) . . . Amen.

3. The Breaking

(Priest hands two parts of the Bread to the Deacons for them to break up)

Priest:
The bread which we break, is not a Communion in the body of Christ.

All:
We who are many are one Bread, one Body, for we all partake of the one bread.
(All kneel)

All:
We do not presume to come to this Thy table worthy. Amen.

By making the fraction a distinct moment, we realize that it is also we who are broken with Christ on the Cross for the life of the world. His sacrifice demands, now symbolically, and then during the week, the sacrifice of our lives.

4. The Sharing

(Priest and Deacons standing)

Priest:
Brethren, this is the joyful and Holy feast of the people of God.

(Three or four rows go up and stand as a group around the table. The Priest hands round the bread and wine saying:)

The Body of Our Lord
    (Blood)

(and then when each group has finished, dismissing them with these words:)

Go in the joy of Jesus Christ
    (peace)
    (love)

(Finally the Priest and Deacons will eat and drink. Then a silence will be kept.)

The Communion is not a private affair, but a public sign, serious certainly, but basically joyous.

Priest:
Father, we thank and priase You for the gift of life, for the gift of Your only Son, whose life, death and rising has freed us from the power of evil and who has caught us up into His new life; and for the gift of Your Spirit to lead all disciples into full obedience and truth. Grant now also to us that we may discern Your purposes, and, forgetting all else, live only for You and for our neighbors, that in the end we may join with all your people in the newness of the whole creation.

All:
(Organ begins immediately, all stand)
Amen.

Hymn: "Thou, Whole Almighty Word"
(Priest and Deacons clear away during the hymn.)

The common has been made holy, we have renewed in faith. Go, then, as did those first disciples, in the power and purpose of Christ's spirit. Go, in peace and in love, sparing nothing of self, but giving and doing all in the name of Jesus, who is Lord.

(He shakes Deacons by the hand. Each person in the congregation shakes hands with his two neighbors, and goes straight out to supper in the hall)

No more blessing is needed after sharing in the Body and the Blood. The service ends with a commission—a sending out to be and to bring about a Holy Communion throughout the week.

Rather than just saying 'Amen,' we commit ourselves, also to one another by the common gesture of a handshake.

Political Involvement

Worship service prepared at the "School on Worship" Ecumenical Christian Centre, Whitefield, Bangalore, December 2nd-8th, 1970. The original ending has been modified. With regard to this service there was a heated discussion, whether a worship service should have a Bible reading and an explicit prayer, or whether this service as it stands is a real worship service.

Scene: While the priest leads the singing of the congregation, a small group stands outside and shouts slogans against injustice.

Song: "Now Thank We All Our God"

Priest: Lord, there they are again; I had been dreading that noise all these days — the noise of the unsatisfied, the noise of the have-nots, the noise of the people who want to topple society. They clamor for justice, equality and shout that the Church should decide which camp she belongs to; politicians have been instigating these people. But Lord, here amidst this assembly of people who lift their hearts to you in peace, I'm confused. You have called me to serve you through the people; am I doing that when I sit on the sidelines and pass judgments on others' actions? Some of your ministers thought it fit to enter party politics; will you castigate their actions or praise them, Lord? All my days in the seminary were filled with the outlook that politics is a dirty game and the Church should never soil her clean hands. Is this possible today, Lord? Can I bring to you the spiritual self without the whole person? I'm confused, Lord, and the noise you've just heard outside, the noise of the political-minded, makes me wonder at my role as your minister.

Voice (of God): Son, my teachings are valued at all times. But they have to be applied without any reservations. I've been incarnated into the world of the 20th century today, and if politics is what rules the world, I should be there, and you, my son, have to immerse yourself in it completely. There are no half measures in my life, and I lived out my life fully, for others. You are my minister, not because you wear that robe, or because people respect you as their spokesman, but because you live out the life of total involvement and dedication as I had done. So have courage, son, but let your heart never rest, till you've set other hearts aflame for this cry for justice and love.

Naxalite: I've sat on this bench for many years, Lord. It is comfortable. There is a peaceful atmosphere all over this place. It is cozy, Lord, to come and relate to you all the good deeds and acts of Christ we've done. But Lord, the real and true picture is the noise you heard outside. My country is torn with different pictures today and I myself have a strong Naxalite outlook. People are dying outside of hunger; many cannot call a piece of land their own; the rich heap the harvest they did not sow; millions have to sleep on the pavements and die like mere animals; yet these rich and affluent people try to pray, as if nothing is wrong; they have their parties, joyful fetes, enjoyable picnics. Is this the way you have shown, Lord? Your doctrine has a revolutionary tone to it and you thrashed out at the cozy "establishment." We who feel one with the Naxalite way of thinking, are convinced, Lord, that this courageous society cannot be repaired. This society is sick, old and like a leper, it does not feel anymore. This society has to be annihilated. Only then, a society based on your justice can become a reality. Violence is the only whip these people understand.

Voice (of God): Isn't it wonderful, son, that I feel that you are more close to me than many people who profess my name? I've come to set fire to the world and only with the help of men like you, I can fulfill this task. Many of my disciples prefer me not to disturb their settled ways. They twist the naked truth I preached. I involved myself fully in the affairs of my country. Anyone who wishes to follow me, has to do this and change society by being a live-wire in this revolution. But son, violence has its repercussions. Can it answer your need? Can it bring the justice you are craving for? I admit at times it is necessary to resort to violence, but remember, son, I always respected persons. Think along this line, son, but I'd like you to keep your fiery aspirations aflame.

Naxalite: It is fine, Lord, to console me with these words. Yet how long can I keep my heart burning with desire for justice? Society will slowly enmesh me with the usual platitudes. The easiest way to live today, Lord, is to conform to established rules. Nothing troubles you then. But I'll never be able to do that. I want to go ahead, even if it means destroying the present society.

Voice (of God): You'll have to act

according to your convictions, son, but act responsibly.

Good Politician: Politicians! Who are we, people trying our hands at each and everything—for better or worse. Lord, you know we are two kinds of people by our own nature, the good and the bad. But both of us think that each group of us are good. If I am a good politician I am more humanistic in my approach to the problem. I see people cry; cry for food, cry for more justice, cry for clothes and shelter, cry for job opportunities and so on. And then nature adding on the problems and calamities, floods, ghastly winds, costing lives and livelihoods. I have only become a victim of this and I am bogged down to the bottom, because I am one with them, sharing my clothes, my food, my wealth, my shelter. I have given everything, whatever I have, and comforted them in their distress. But Lord, I still have to do more. I feel as if I have not done anything at all.

Voice (of God): Truly I say unto you, inasmuch as you have done it unto one of the least of these my brethren, you have done it unto me.

Bad Politician: See me, Lord, I am a bad politician, but I still think that I am good and behave differently. I also see and am confronted with all these problems. But I cannot commit myself to solving them, especially when I have my own problems. If someone suffers it may be because he did not save anything himself; it may be his fate or his sins. I need to have money and wealth. Not only should I fulfill the needs of those of my dependents, I must also look respectable in society. Look at the power I enjoy and my prestige. By some means I need to keep them up. I also give charities, loans, subscribe more to the Church than others. I sometimes preach, pray and make eloquent speeches. What do you think of that?

Voice (of God): Curse be unto you, Scribes and Pharisees, hypocrites! For you have paid attention to the materialistic side of life, and have omitted weightier matters of law, judgment, mercy and faith, these you ought to have done and not to leave the others undone.

Student: Down with Hindi — Down with Expo '70 — help Lord, I'm confused — what is expected of me? Where do I turn? Which side do I take, Lord? If I am where the "establishment" is, I feel a traitor to the student community. But then, Lord, if I do not usually agree with what the students agitate for, is it imperative that I join with them to be a part of them? I must be active, if I wish the world to proceed—but action so often means violence. I am afraid, Lord, to be violent, when I think of the harm it may cause. And then again, Lord, I am apathetic. I do not want to be involved, because so much is expected of me. I do not wish to get out of this complacency and act, Lord, this is my plea, tell me what your will is, for when I see the confusion, poverty and destruction that exist in my college campus, I know that this is not your will.

Voice (of God): It is my will, my son. Go into your campus and see that I am there. How can you be complacent, how can you accept things as they are, when you know that they are not right? Why don't you try to lead a "real" life?

Student: It is strange, Lord, how complicated your world has become. I really know that you did not want it to be that way. It is my fault. Sometimes I become desperate, when I find how we run around in a vicious circle of unsolved problems, we poor, crazy creatures. The whole show must look rather ridiculous to you. It must take a lot of patience on your side to continue to take our world seriously in spite of all. Forgive me, Lord, and teach me what to do.

The Illiterate: Lord, I am a farmer. I have not gone to school. When the time of election comes, I only feel I must elect someone who will lead us. So I go for the voting, I place my thumb impression and vote for the person who is talked of by many people, or for the symbol which fits in with my way of life. I do not know whether I am right or wrong. But what satisfies me is that I have my responsible job of electing a leader. But, Lord, I begin to wonder when I see the educated, responsible citizens of India behave irresponsibly. During the elections they go about as if it does not concern them at all. I am worried about the elections, because we need a man who can uplift the well-being of many. But the educated rich man is not disturbed a bit, because he is already well-off and he seems to think that he knows more than the ordinary politicians. He is ready to vote for the one who will enrich him more. That is what some of my fellow men who are educated, educated to be responsible, do. But I keep wondering, Lord.

Voice (of God): My son, I am glad you wonder. I like people who get involved. But I snicker at those who do not commit themselves completely to the task in which they are involved.

You remember the widow in the Gospel, who gave all that she had without expecting anything in return. So be of good cheer and carry on being involved. What you do may be little, but be involved in where you need to be involved.

Priest: Lord, you have heard my congregation struggling with your will. More than ever we realize that we are pilgrims, traveling toward your kingdom. Make us truly honest in our search for your will, deliver us from confusing your will with our own selfish one, so that we become true messengers of you, who are Love.

Please, bless us, our search and our struggle.

May the Grace of our Lord Jesus Christ,

the Love of God and the Fellowship of the Holy Spirit,

be with us all now and for ever.
AMEN
Song

To The Westerners

Shanmugha Subbiah

On the one hand you devise
ways of living well;
on the other you dig
graves with consummate knowledge.

We do not have zest for life
We do not dare to die
We are not like you
We live without living
We die without dying
We are we.

Shanmugha Subbiah is a "major voice" in the Tamil literary tradition. Below is the Tamil translation.

மேற்கத்தியோரே

ஒரு பக்கம்
வாழ வழிவகுக்கும்
மறு பக்கம்
சாகக் குழிபறிக்கும்
உங்களைப் போலல்ல
நாங்கள்.
நாங்களோ
வாழவும் விரும்ப மாட்டோம்
சாகவும் துணிய மாட்டோம்.
உங்களைப் போலல்ல
நாங்கள்.
வாழாமல் வாழ்ந்து
சாகாமற் சாகும்
நாங்கள் நாங்களே.

Conference on 'The Unmasking of Man: Marx and Freud'

Introduction

The sources of the material used in this act, in addition to extracts from Marx, Freud and Christian Scripture, include the writings of T.S. Eliot and the songs of Sydney Carter. The music to one of the hymns, and both the words and the music of the Secular Anthem were composed by students at the Conference.

The purpose of this act is to recall the divisions we experience in contemporary life, and the understanding by Marx, Freud and Jesus Christ of these divisions; and also, to affirm the answers these three men provided as tools for tackling the problems.

We do not want to diminish Marx or Freud by implying that Jesus himself taught their ideas before them; not do we want to suggest that the teachings of Marx and of Freud are useless without the teachings of Jesus.

We do want this act to express our acute awareness of a world of divisions, and to affirm the concern of Marx, Freud and Jesus Christ that these divisions should be healed.

The motif of the act is the three-fold separation experienced by a man of this age:

(1) his alienation from other men
(2) his conflicts within himself
(3) his separation from God

Part 1. What is Man? — The unmasking of man

Reading: "We are the Hollow Men" from T. S. Eliot's "The Wasteland"
Confession:

V. We confess that we are restless, divided in ourselves:
R. We are complacent about the divisions in our world.
V. We find it hard to distinguish the real from the substitute:
R. Often we prefer not to.
V. We justify ourselves when we act irresponsibly:
R. We fear the freedom that comes with forgiveness.
V. We are alienated from one another:
R. Uneasy with the realization that life is related to You.

Leader: We confess that we like to believe that the more we learn, the more we know; we dare not admit our ignorance:
FORGIVE US our learning—we mistake it for Truth.

We confess that we like to believe that all men are brothers; we dare not admit we are not prepared to do anything about a world of inequality:
FORGIVE US the charitable smile, the comforting resolution—we mistake them for love.

We confess that we like to believe ourselves persons of integrity and responsibility; we dare not admit our Jeckel and Hyde existence:
FORGIVE US the stiff upper-lip—we mistake it for an expression of ourselves.

We confess that we like to think God is always running after us; we dare not admit that we are not prepared to deny ourselves and take up our Cross daily:
FORGIVE US our piety—we mistake it for loving God with heart, mind, soul and strength.

V. Lord, have mercy
R. Christ, have mercy.

CLOSING ACT OF WORSHIP

V. Lord, have mercy.

Reading from MARX (from Critique of Hegel's "Philosophy of Right")

"Man makes religion, religion does not make man. Religion is indeed man's self-consciousness and self-awareness as long as he has not found his feet in the universe. But man is not an abstract being, squatting outside the world. Man is the world of men, the State and society. This State, this society, produce religion which is an inverted world consciousness, because they are an inverted world. Religion is the general theory of this world, its encyclopedic compendium, its logic in popular form, its spiritual *point d'honneur*, its enthusiasm, its moral sanction, its solemn complement, its general basis of consolation and justification. It is the fantastic realization of the human being inasmuch as human being possesses no true reality. The struggle against religions is therefore indirectly a struggle against that world whose spiritual aroma is religion.

"Religious suffering is at the same time an expression of real suffering and a protest against real suffering. Religion is the sigh of the oppressed creature, the sentiment of a heartless world, and the soul of soulless conditions. It is the opium of the people. The abolition of religion, as the illusory happiness of men, is a demand for their real happiness. The call to abandon their illusions about their condition is a call to abandon a condition which requires illusions. . . . The immediate task is to unmask human alienation in its secular form, now that it has been unmasked in its sacred form. Thus the criticism of heaven transforms itself into the criticism of earth, the criticism of religion into the criticism of law, and the criticism of theology into the criticism of politics."

Reading from FREUD (from "The Question of Lay-Analysis")

"It is easy now to describe our therapeutic aim. We try to restore the ego, to free it from its restrictions, and to give it back the command over the id which it has lost owing to its early repressions. It is for this one purpose that we carry out analysis, our whole technique is directed to this aim. We have to seek out the repressions which have been set up and to urge the ego to correct them with our help and to deal with conflicts better than by an attempt at flight. Since these repressions belong to the very early years of childhood, the work of analysis leads us, too, back to that period. Our path to these situations of conflict, which have for the most part been forgotten and which we try to revive in the patient's memory, is pointed out to us by his symptoms, dreams and free associations. These must, however, first be interpreted—translated—for, under the influence of the psychology of the id, they have assumed forms of expression that are strange to our comprehension. . . . By encouraging the patient to disregard his resistances to telling us these things, we are educating his ego to overcome its inclination towards attempts at flight and to tolerate an approach to what is repressed. In the end, if the situation of the repression can be successfully reproduced in his memory, his compliance will be brilliantly rewarded. The whole difference between his age then and now works in his favor: and the thing from which his childish ego fled in terror will often seem to his adult and strengthened ego no more than child's play."

Psalm 139, verses 1-11 (read antiphonally)

PART 2: Who Do Men Say That I Am? — The Unmasking of God

Song: "It's God They Ought to Crucify" Chorus (sung together):
It's God they ought to crucify instead of you and me,
I said to the carpenter a'hanging on the tree.

Scripture: Mark 15, verses 21-39

Sermon:

The Commandments of the Lord Jesus (with responses)

PART 3: What Shall We Answer? — The Unmasking of Me

Hymn: "The Head That Once Was Crowned With Thorns" (Tune: John Truss)

Intercessions

Let us pray for those suffering in Vietnam. For U Thant and those seeking a peaceful solution there.

For Bishop Ambrose Reeves and Pastor Niemoller and others visiting and identifying themselves with the peoples in Vietnam.

For all those deeply concerned with the problem. For American students in their attitudes to the policies of their governments and all imprisoned for refusing to fight in Vietnam.

V. Lord do something about it.

R. And show us what to do.

For divisions caused by men in their search for truth.

For the ecumenical movement and those involved in its work.

For us and all others confronted by our inability to participate in a common Eucharist.

For those torn between loyalty to Christ and allegiance to the church order.

For the S.C.M., for the executive committee, general council and David Head.

For those whom the church neglects to serve while she is absorbed in her own internal strife.

V. Lord do something about it.

R. And show us what to do.

For the divisions caused within men by their lack of understanding of themselves.

For us, at this conference, when we have to make important decisions and are frightened to commit ourselves.

For us, as we attempt to communicate with one another in a meaningful way.

For us, that we can take the responsibility of being the Student Christian Movement.

For the whole of mankind, that, in a divided world it can bear to struggle on towards peace.

For each one of us that he may be true to himself.

V. Lord do something about it.

R. And show us what to do.

Offering (The money had already been put into baskets on the table, designated as follows:

Present visit of Bishop Reeves and others to Vietnam,

Immediate medical relief for Vietnam, Vietnam Action Group, and possibly a student delegation to Vietnam, S.C.M. Associate Forms with promises.)

Dedication:

Secular Anthem (Choir): "Hull Power Station"

'No thanks!' to the corny analogy
'PRAYER IS THE POWERHOUSE OF GOD';
but Amen! to the thick concave chimney
a sign, like the Mosaic rod,
of the caring of God for His people,
the sharing of Jesus the carpenter's Son:
this chimney that towers from that flat panorama
the skyline of Hull,
long, level, and dull,
like a Sinai billowing steam in the heavens
while the flame-colored dawn-disc, the sun,
burns coldly upon the thin lip
of the great concrete crater;
a pillar of cloud and of fire,
and symbol of God, the Creator.

(Chris Blackwell)

Affirmation from Marx ("Theses on Feuerbach")

"The educator must himself be educated.... The real nature of man is the totality of social relations.... The standpoint of the old type of materialism is civil society; the standpoint of the new materialism is human society or social humanity.... The philosophers have only *interpreted* the world in different ways; the point is to change it."

Affirmation from Freud: (slightly adapted from "Civilization and its Discontents").

"The fateful question for the human species seems to me to be whether and to what extent their cultural development will succeed in mastering the disturbance of their communal life by the human instinct of aggression and self-destruction. It may be that in this respect precisely the present time deserves a special interest. Men have gained control over the forces of nature to such an extent that with their help they would have no difficulty in exterminating one another to the last man. They know this, and hence comes a large part of their current unrest, their unhappiness and their mood of anxiety. And now it is to be expected that eternal Life will make an effort to assert himself in the struggle with his equally immortal adversary, Death."

Affirmation from Jesus Christ

"Jesus answered, 'in truth, in very truth I tell you, unless a man has been born over again he cannot see the kingdom of God.' 'But how is it possible,' said Nicodemus, 'for a man to be born when he is old? Can he enter his mother's womb a second time and be born?' Jesus answered, 'The wind blows where it will; you hear the sound of it, but you do not know where it comes from, or where it is going. So with everyone who is born from spirit.' Nicodemus replied, 'How is this possible?' " (John 3, verses 3-9)

Hymn: "Forth In Thy Name"

Prayer (Vespers of German Lutheran Church—said together)

Abide with us, Lord, for it is toward evening and the day is far spent.

Abide with us and with thy whole Church.

Abide with us in the end of the day, in the end of our life, and in the end of the world.

Abide with us with thy grace and bounty, with thy holy Word and Sacrament, with thy comfort and thy blessing.

Abide with us when over us cometh the night of affliction and fear, the night of doubt and temptation, the night of bitter death.

Abide with us, and with all thy faithful, through time and eternity. Amen.

Blessing:

V. Into your hands we commend this conference:

R. We commend ourselves.

V. The peace of the Lord be always with you:

R. With you, and with all. Amen.

Answer to the Question From Our Left-Wing Friends On Why We Pray

Because it is for us a matter of the brotherhood of all,
Not only of Christians or another group but all,
All those who will live after us
In our towns with our water
Brought up by us to the third and fourth generations
Of all
Of the dead who lived before us
Whose dreams we have betrayed
The dreams of 1789 and those of 1917
Because our brothers are of concern to us

> That is why we sometimes say
> OUR FATHER

Because our task is unending
And our longing does not grow less
In the course of our lives
Because Christ does not quench our thirst
But makes it greater

> That is why we sometimes say
> WHO ART IN HEAVEN

Because we live in places
Where people have to talk about people
In factories, offices and schools
Because we know that dominion is
The commonest way
To offend the name of God

> That is why we sometimes say
> HALLOWED BE THY NAME

Because we fear the cycle
Of production, consumption and profit
To which they want to train us up

> That is why we sometimes say
> THY WILL BE DONE

Because we are not without fear
Of ourselves too
Not without doubt, in ourselves too
And our way
Not without derision for our own experiments too

> That is why we sometimes say
> THY KINGDOM COME

We speak of daily bread
And mean the button that the
Prisoner in the cell lacks
And the low duty on goods
From other countries.

We confess our guilt
As one of the richest people of the earth,
Which is full of the starving,
As citizens of a well-ordered land,
That is full of those in despair.

We forgive our debtors
Who are cheating us out of our lives
Because we do not cease
To make better suggestions to them
Thus respecting their dignity.

Because we are German Germans
Blind with nationalism and
Sick with the desire for revenge
Because we do not recognize whole countries
And will not acknowledge frontiers or peace

> That is why we sometimes say
> AND LEAD US NOT
> INTO TEMPTATION

Because we are submissive
And have not learnt
To set limits to dominion
And to control the powerful
And still scarcely understand
How to share in planning our destiny
Because we abandon ourselves
To resignation and blind grief

> That is why we sometimes say
> BUT DELIVER US FROM EVIL

Because we need faith for the Kingdom
Which we are and which we are building
And encouragement for our work
So that we do not plan in vain

> That is why we sometimes say
> THINE IS THE KINGDOM,
> THE POWER AND THE GLORY

And stake our faith that God is
IN ETERNITY for us.

Prayer

Halina Bortnowska

It would surely be good
if now and then we could look into
   Paradise
and meet God like a friend
under the trees in the evening air.

Then we could discuss
this or that with him
in a friendly atmosphere.
We could tell him the news from the
   world,
what he should change
so that we could really be pleased with it.

All history,
not just the history of the Cross,
but that, too, and that above all
stops my dictating to God
what he should do.

So my prayer takes the form of pain
at the fact that my heart, my home and
   my city
do not reflect the splendor of existence,
the ground and source of which is God.

These are things, God, of which you
   alone are Lord.
These you bestow, I know,
with boundless and incomprehensible
   generosity.
The greatest of them is love,
hope's sister, the companion on our way.
If I open my eye
You can remove the plank from it.

But beyond that,
you have left the organization of the
   world to us.
There is no point in repeating:
O God, give, remember, do—

We are the ones who have to give, do
   and remember
and then say: we are worthless servants.
Here is our body and the work of our
   hands,
brittle, bitty, unfinished.
Through them we tried to express
something that defies all expression and
   to which
you are calling us.

This prayer was offered during worship in a group of Polish, East German and Czech Christians who met in October 1971 to share with each other their experiences and experiments in developing new forms of Christian presence in their respective societies.

Friendship

1. **Preparation:**
   Each participant brings a flower; the participants sit in a circle; in the middle of the circle is put a table.

2. **Introduction:**
   We have come to worship as a community. Let us make manifest our friendship for one another by offering our flowers on the community table. Let us ponder in this service on the community spirit that exists between us and dedicate ourselves to the greatness of this friendship.
   (The participants rise and put their flowers on the community table in the center.)

3. **Incidents of everyday life:**
   (Four participants relate different experiences of friendship)
   - Friendship and community living
   - Friendship and loyalty
   - Friendship and mutual love, acceptance and openness
   - Friendship and giving advice, help and support, etc.

4. **Bible Reading: John 15:9-17**
   Friendship means giving oneself, laying down one's life for the other(s).

5. **Reflection:**
   i) a period of silence
   ii) after this period of silence some of the participants spontaneously share their reflection with the others. They relate both the incidents given (no. 3) and the Bible reading to their own life. (If the community or group is not accustomed to this spontaneous sharing of reflections in a worship service or the group is large, it is good to ask and prepare a few people beforehand.)

6. **Penitential prayer:**
   The group spontaneously formulates their prayer for forgiveness in the light of the service up to now, e.g. for misunderstanding our friends, for not taking their advice, for lack of loyalty, etc. (What is put between parentheses in no. 5 also holds good here.)

7. **The prayer "Simon of Cyrene"**
   "And led him away to be crucified. As for his cross, they forced a passer-by who was coming in from the country to carry it, one Simon of Cyrene" (Mark 15: 20-21).
   He passed by on the road;
   They pressed him into service
   The first to come along, a stranger.
   Lord, you accepted his help.
   You did not want the help of a friend, the solace of a gesture of love,
   the generous impulse of one who cared.
   You chose the enforced help of an indifferent and timid fellow.
   Lord All-Powerful, you sought the help of a powerless man.
   By your own choosing you are in need of us.
   Lord, I need others.
   The way of man is too hard to be trodden alone.
   But I avoid the hands outstretched to help me,
   I want to act alone,
   I want to fight alone,
   I want to succeed alone.
   And yet beside me walks a friend, a spouse, a brother, a neighbor, a fellow-worker.
   You have placed them near me, Lord, and too often I ignore them.
   And yet it is together that we shall save the world.
   Lord, even if they are requisitioned, grant that I may see, that I may accept, all the Simons on my road.

8. **Greeting:**
   There are many ways in which friendship can be expressed—a handshake, a smile, a kiss. Let us in this community look around us at the friendship that does exist around us and express it by greeting one another in that way which can be most informal and meaningful to us. (Participants move around among themselves, greeting each other, then all go back to their places.)
   As a symbol of our affection for one another let us give each other a flower. A wild flower whose growth does not need to be nurtured, but which grows wildly and unheedingly—like a friendly nature that grows in us without any necessity, if we give it chance to grow. (The participants go to the table and give one of the flowers to the neighbor on their right hand.)

9. **Blessing:** (all together)
   May the Lord bless us and guard us,
   Show his face to us and have mercy on us,
   turn his face toward us and give us peace.
   May the Lord bless us. Amen.

Worship service, prepared by the participants of the "School on Worship," Ecumenical Christian Centre, Whitefield, Bangalore, 1970 (slightly adapted).

African Eucharist

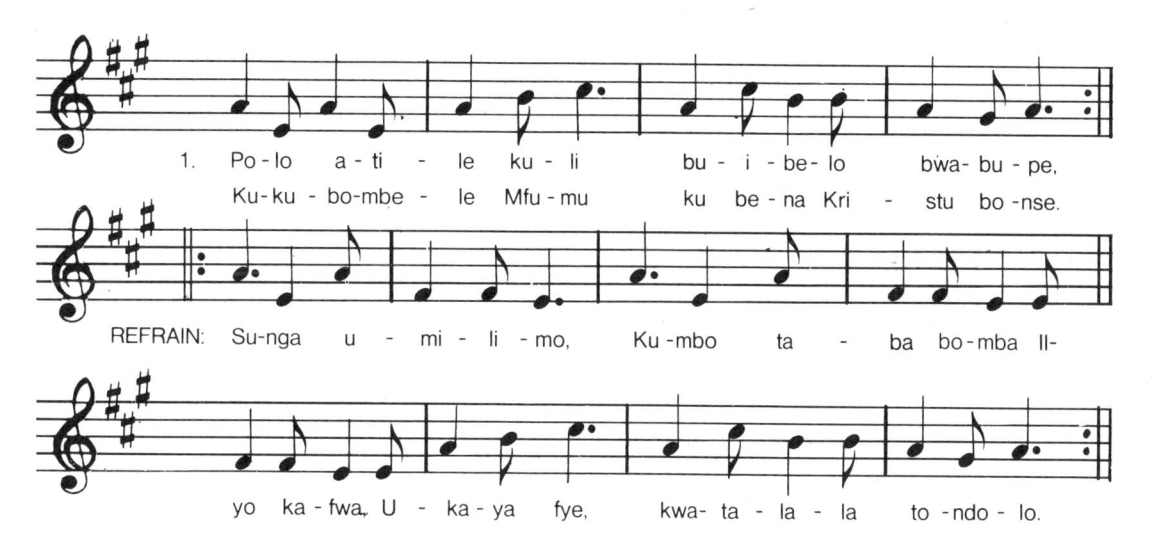

PROCESSIONAL HYMN

ZAMBIA — Bemba
Ronald Ndawa

1. Po-lo a-ti-le ku-li bu-i-be-lo bwa-bu-pe,
Ku-ku-bo-mbe-le Mfu-mu ku be-na Kri-stu bo-nse.

REFRAIN: Su-nga u-mi-li-mo, Ku-mbo ta-ba bo-mba Il-yo ka-fwa, U-ka-ya fye, kwa-ta-la-la to-ndo-lo.

Bemba text:

1. Polo atile kuli buibelo bwabupe,
   Ku kubombele Mfumu ku bena Kristu bonse.

   REFRAIN:
   Sunga umilimo Kumbo taba bomba ilyo kafwa,
   Ukaya fye, kwatalala tondolo.

2. Imilimo twapelwa tusunge no kucita,
   Pantu lintu twaleka, twalufya icilambu.

3. Fwe baleka milimo intu Lesa atupa,
   Twibukishe ukuti calo cili nekupwa.

4. Nga uli kashimika wileko kushimika,
   E mulimo wa Mfumu untu Lesa atupa.

5. Amatalanta yobe yalefwaikwe lelo,
   Ni abo basumina pa mulandu wa iwe.

English translation: (Not to be sung)

1. Paul said there are diversities of gifts.
   Christians, serve the Lord.

   REFRAIN:
   Praise the Lord when you are alive,
   For the dead do not praise Him.

2. Let us keep and do the work we are given,
   for when we fail to do it we lose our Crown of Life.

3. We who have stopped the work which God gave us
   Should remember that the world will come to an end.

4. Do not stop preaching if you are a preacher,
   That is the very work which God has given you.

5. God wants your talents,
   There are those who believe because of your work.

Leader: God, who leads your people out of slavery into the glorious liberty of the children of God.

P: Set us free.

L: St. Paul says, "Like men rescued from certain death, put yourselves in God's hands as weapons of good for his own purposes. For sin is not meant to be your master—you are no longer living under law but under grace."

And this freedom I proclaim to you at the command of our Lord, Jesus Christ, in the name of the Father, Son and Holy Spirit.

P: Amen.

Reading of Scripture and Sermon
Song
Turku Affirmation of Faith: (said by all)
The good news came in Jesus Christ;
He was the Father's token of what man may be,
He revealed to us what we are—children of God,
He went about bringing joy to life,
He gave himself, as he shared bread and fish with the poor,
As he handed bread and wine to his friends.
So completely did he give himself
That he died on the cross,
He was the messiah who overcame death and lives in eternity.
His death we preach every time we are together.
His resurrection we profess as we stand by our neighbor.
His return we expect when we build the world of tomorrow.
We know we have received his strength through the baptism of water and the spirit:
It is that spirit which makes us the Church, God's people,
Which inspires the world,
And leads it to its ultimate end.

Intercession: (spontaneous)

End all prayers with ". . . we pray to the Lord."
Answer: "O Lord hear our prayer."

Thanksgiving:
Gathered together here
we offer our thanks
for all that we are.
As we stand together
we bring to mind
the continuing life
of Christ.
We recall his simple
beginnings and
life as an
artisan.
We bring to mind his
preaching and works,
signs of his presence
among us.
We recall above
all the moment
when he made his stand
for freedom.
That moment in which
he was condemned to
die.
For that reason we
recall him being
nailed up on
the gallows.
For in that he did
not die but
conquer death
in new life.
Thus in his continuing
life we recall how
the night before he
died
(Gather together as
he now is
among us)
he took bread
into his hands
and said
breaking the bread
this is my body
broken for you
take and eat.
At the end of this meal
he took a cup and said:
drink all of you
this is the cup of my blood
poured out for you
and for all men.

People:
We therefore recall together
Christ's death and resurrection.
Gathered together in one body,
may remain so
in one spirit, the spirit
of love.

Kiss of Peace: (greet each other by name)

Song

Unity in Diversity

World Conference on Salvation Today — Bangkok, Thailand

Order of Service with Notes
Call to Worship:
Songs by Belafonte & Makeba

These are protest songs out of the Southern African situation. The words are *Tula Mama Tula*—quiet mother, quiet—meant to comfort a weeping broken hearted mother whose son has been jailed for "being man."

Be Hleli Bonke Etologwene: There they are (the leaders of the nation) all locked up in prison. Oh, what shall we Africans do! Is there any hope for us?

Announcement of Theme for the Worship Service

Unity in Diversity: In Africa God is experienced by various names among different peoples: Lesa, Mungu, Unkulunkulu, Tixo, Zambe, Mudzimu, yet it is acknowledged that He is the One God. Now it can even be said, "The Father of Our Lord Jesus Christ," "Ruler of the Universe," "Destiny of Mankind."

Intercessions

Therefore all mankind comes to Him saying, "out of the Depth I cry unto Thee O Lord."

Hymn

Let us praise the Lord in song: "O Seigneur, Notre Diem"

Silence

Let us listen to the Lord: "The Lord is in His temple, let all the earth keep silent!"

Scripture: Ephesians 2: 1-10

Meditation

Jer. 31: 15-17, by Mme R. Andriamanjeto. The idea is to remind the world that the majority of church membership in Africa is people of the feminine sex. Also the leadership of the local churches is mainly in the hands of women.

Hymn

"Love Divine All Love's Excelling," to the Xhosa tune:

> Nkosi yan ubongelanda
> Ekulablekweni kwan
> Nkosi yam wamane ulanda
> emkonlweni wam
> Nda funyanwa nkosi yam.

Silence

Let us again keep silent before God. (The music in the background came from the Eglise Evangelique Protestante du Cameroun. They tell how "The enemies of God are sad because Christ has won a victory" and "How we are free.")

Agape Prayer

Grace for the mid-day meal.

The Brotherly Greeting

We all sang a chorus from Kenya meaning "Peace, peace be with you all." Shake hands each with a neighbor.

Dismissal

In silence we proceed to the dining hall. The silence is broken only when in "the breaking of the bread," we say the word of peace and share God's gift of bread with others.

Good-bye

Hallelujah! Hallelujah!	hurrah! hurrah!
We must say today	brother good-bye,
Back to your land!	thank you! thank you!
Good-bye, we rejoice	you'll never come again—
With such pretense	to know God too well!
For why did you say	our tunes did not contain—
The glory of God?	Gosh! Good-bye! Hurrah!
Our rhythms to spring	the Lord needs them.
Why did you frown	when we took the robe:
To dress like the Son?	and you said things—
That the robe matched not	worn on black!
For the Son was white	as if, and really so—
Whiteness was the Son	and blackness the devil!
Why did you not tell us	the shades of Heaven,
If you know too well	the color of the throne,
And the color of the skin	of our dear Lord?
Now we say, Hallelujah!	in the African rhythm;
We'll dance to a stoop	to reach the ground,
And shoulders will shake	like tender branches;
Let's dance to the rhythm	of our black breeze;
Hallelujah!	in the African beat,
In the songs we know	those tunes we make,
To reach our hearts	to convey the delight,
To give the Lord a change	too long He's waited;
Hallelujah!	and hurrah!
Which land shall we find	without His footprint?
Which tune shall we choose	to reach His heart
In what pitch	and in which time—
Must we choose	and be sure to reach Him?
Brother, don't be amazed	they belong to one—
The branches of one tree	and just remember:
The goal is only one	to please the Lord;
We'll keep the paths	cleared and swept—
For the Lord to walk	to enjoy the gardens,
Of Africa	Hallelujah!
Our rivers will flow	our breeze will kiss—
With the breath of the Lord	Hallelujah!
Our mountains will rise	to the glory of God;
For the sky is not less blue	in our Africa;
Our valleys will abound	with the glory of God,
For the sun shines no less	in our Africa.

A Handful Of Prayers

The Traps

Lord,

I wish you would send me
    to a distant land
to an alien people
whose tongue I may take
    years to learn
and whose culture I may
    never fully appreciate.
But I will be at an advantage—
I may throw suggestions
chalk out programs
initiate policies
without ever fearing that
the process of cultural change
    may affect me

But here I am Lord.

A minister to my own people
part of the world I seek to transform
every word I speak
and every move I make
may well touch their lives and mine.
But the complex cultural traps
which outside eyes don't see
gape at me from every side
and challenge me to betray them.
So with measured steps
I leave the troubled spots
and feign I serve you
in truth and dignity
by leading the faithful at worship
praying over the sick
marrying the young
and burying the dead.
But I am sick at heart Lord
when I remember the prophets of old
men who sought to bring to
    repentance
their own kith and kin—
and there is the example
    of your Son Himself who
came unto His own
to break open doors which
    tradition had shut
and let Thy grace shine through.

So
I ask of you Lord
if it is your wish
that I serve my own people
give me a double portion of
    your spirit
that I may expose
and condemn in your Name
every evil which distorts human life
and truly seek to set my people free.

Drop-Out

Lord,
I want to be a drop-out
I want to stand by
    the roadside
watch people go by,
speak to them
find out what they are,
what they are after,
know what life is
and choose for myself
    the path I'll tread.

Lord,
I want to be a drop-out
I want to see places,
meet new people
scale mountains
cross oceans
and make my own
the knowledge
which closed pages hold.

Lord,
I want to be a drop-out
that I may know
what I can become
and not believe
what they say
I can be,
or worse still,
become what they want me to be.

Lord,
I want to be a drop-out
stop running with the crowd
though only for a while—
stand out and scale
the past and the present
look beyond the known
and lay hold on life
which Thy spirit whispers
is mine
if only I may seek
to possess it.

Lord, I am Twenty-five!

Lord!
I am twenty-five!
Time I got married
But I do not belong to a culture
which gives a woman the freedom
to choose her own mate
neither do I form
part of the traditional world
where parents make the choice
with pious care
worse still,
my father has turned "religious"
he refuses to pay the bride-money
this is sin; this is against the law
    of the land he says,
and seeks to save his soul—

While I
daily take my books
fight my way through electric train or bus
and loose myself in a school,
    college or office
working, to take back the
    pay-packet
at the month's end to my
    father—
this is what dutiful
    daughters are supposed to do!

Thus while I pass my days,
no angel comes to greet me
and pronounce me blessed
this I do not regret,
For I seek not to fulfill
a special mission—
grant me Lord, the normal
    natural wish
to be a wife, a mother—
to have a home of my own—
to cook a meal, and make
    a bed—

While life and its patterns change
let thine immortal Hand
show us the way Lord,
to make life meaningful,
    lovable and real—
even as structures which crush
    the human spirit be pulled
    down and destroyed—
cause new forms and shapes to arise
which may truly reflect
Thy love and tenderness to
    fallen man.

The Thief

Father,
They lead my people astray!
When the rich exploit the poor
The learned cheat the ignorant
The politician lies to the voter
And the vendor uses false weight
I understand,
This is the way of the world
I keep myself on guard.

But this evil I confront
Is too sinister, Lord,
To betray its ugly form
To untrained eyes.

This man I know of
Makes religion his "business."
He entices the emotionally sick
With promises of health
And eternal rest in heaven;
Then robs them of their wit
And leaves them—
Deathly shadows—to their bitter end.

Lord I confess that
This weakness is in our blood
For long ages we let the
Religious rule over us
Among our sages, monks and Sadus
Were many a wolf
Which had without a thought
Devoured the sheep.
And to this evil
We again become a prey
In the name of the lord
Who banished the middle man
And tore the curtain through.

Lord,
Cause my people to awake
Let them listen to the voice
Which speaks to them not in
Thunder, earthquake or fire
But in stillness softness and love
That the precious gift of reason
May not be trampled upon
But remain
At Thy altar
A living glowing flame.

Latin American Lord's Prayer

our Father who art in heaven
with the swallows and the missiles
I want you back before you forget
how to reach South of the Rio Grande

our Father in exile
you almost never remember my people
anyway wherever you are
hallowed by thy name
not those who hallow in your name
closing an eye so as not to see fingernails
filthy with wretchedness

in august of nineteen sixty
it doesn't work anymore to ask that
thy kingdom come to us
because your kingdom is down here too
stuck in the anger and fear
in irresolutions and in filth
in disillusionment and in lethargy
in the eagerness to see you
    in spite of it all

when you spoke of the rich man
the needle and the camel
and we all unanimously voted
you into glory
the silent respectful Indian
    raised his hand too
but refused to think thy will be done
nonetheless once in a while
your will gets tangled up with mine
overcomes it
enflames it
multiplies it

it's harder to know what my will is
when I really believe what I say that I
    believe
in your omnipresence as in my solitude
on earth as it is in heaven
always
i'll feel safer about the ground I walk on

than the manageable heaven ignorant of
    me
but who knows
I'm not going to decide
that your will be done or undone
your will is being done anyway in the
    wind
in the snowy Andes
in the bird who fertilizes his mate
in chancelors who mumble "yes sir" in
    english
in each hand turned into a fist

of course I'm not sure I like the way
your will chooses to be done
I say so with irreverence and gratitude
two characters that soon will be one
I say so thinking especially of our daily
bread and each little piece of day
yesterday you took it from us
give it to us this day
or at least give us the right to our bread
not just the bread which was a symbol of
    something
but also the bread with a soft part and
    crust
our bread

now that we have few hopes and debts
    left
forgive us our debts if you can
but don't forgive us our hopes
don't even forgive us our credits

tomorrow at the latest
we'll go out and collect from the double-
    dealers
tangible, smiling outlaws
from those who have claws for harp-
    playing
and a Panamerican quivering with which
    they wipe off
the last drool that hangs from their face

it doesn't matter if our creditors forgive
as we
once
by mistake
forgave our debtors

still
they owe us about a century
of sleeplessness and clubbing
about three thousand miles of insults
adout twenty medals to Somoza
about one single dead Guatemala
don't let us fall into the temptation
of forgetting or selling that past
or leasing a single acre of its memory

now that it's the moment of knowing
    who we are
and the dollar and his unredeeming love
are to cross the river
tear out from our soul the last beggar
and save us from remorse

—Mario Benedetti
—translated by Mary Jane Wilkie

Lament for The June Sun

Abdul Wahab al-Bayati

We are pounded in the cafe of the East†
War of words
Wooden swords
Lies and horsemen of the air.
We did not kill a camel or a crow:
We did not try the game of death:
We did not play with knights or even
    pawns:
Our employment trivia
As we slew each other to the final crumb.
In the cafe of the East we swat at flies.
We wear the mask of life in history's
    garbage can,
Aping men.
We dared not bell the cat, even at its tail.
We did not ask the blind deceiver: why
    did you escape?
We are the generation of profitless death,
Recipients of alms.
Our defeat in the cafe of the East: the
    war of words,
The peacocks‡ strutting the halls where
    pride is dead,
The essays of obedient hacks
Staining pages
Staining the shoes of the powerful
With the blood of truth.
We are the generation of profitless deaths
    and alms.
We neither died nor were born
Nor knew the anguish of heroes.

Why did they leave us in the waste?
O my God the predatory birds
We pull on the tatters of our dead and
    weep without shame.
No rag for our nakedness is left by the
    June sun.
Why do they leave us to the dogs
Corpses without prayer
Bearing the murdered nation in one fist
    and dust in the other?

Don't brush the flies from the wound
My wound is Job's mouth
My pain consists in waiting
My blood seeks vengeance.

O God of the poor toilers
We were not defeated: but the giant
    peacocks
They were defeated and they only
Quicker than the lighting of a match.

Abdul Wahab al-Bayati was born in 1926 in Baghdad but has lived most of his adult life outside Iraq, first in Moscow, then in Damascus and Cairo.

† A center for intellectuals
‡ An allusion to the Arab leaders

Short Prayers

A

Lord, I just don't know what to say when I am asked to make a prayer.
It is like being asked to breathe.

B

O God, our Creator!
We thank you for your continuous act of creation.
Thank you, for creating new societies in the world,
societies, which stand above the caste-ridden and the color-ridden society and
we ask that the new society may be delivered from inequality.

We thank you for the new forms of worship
and we ask that these forms
will neither exclude the vertical nor the horizontal dimensions
of human life.
We thank you for the inventions of science
and the knowledge it brings forth about the universe;
and we ask that this knowledge be dedicated to realize your
Kingdom on earth and not a technocracy, that does not respect man—young or old, feeble or brave.

God, we thank you for revealing yourself in your Son Jesus
Christ—the man for others.
May the love of Jesus Christ flood our country and the world
at large that our attitudes may be attuned to His,
and thus bring peace and prosperity on earth.

God, we thank you for the work of the Holy Spirit
which cannot be limited to the church.
We pray that the Spirit may draw all men together
to Jesus Christ, our Lord and Savior.
                                      Amen

C

O God!
When I begin to pray I most of all want to say: Thank you!
No wonder you saw that things were good.
They are good.
The world is so amazingly beautiful in many ways.
Butterflies, for instance. How many varieties there are!
The sunsets and (when I see them) the dawns and sunrises.
Each day different and each one a masterpiece in this country,
except for about two days per annum.
Thank you!

Then music.
Music says far more than words can do.
Thank you for Palestrina and Bach and Mozart.
Thank you for madrigals and singing itself.
Thank you for the new songs that I like, and help me to like the ones I don't,
if you think they will be helpful to those I can teach them to.
But, of course, even more beautiful things to see are sounds to
                                      hear—
suppose, I were deaf and blind,
which I hope in your mercy I won't be, or at least not until I'm
                                      extremely ancient.
Thank you for people.
Thank you for optimists and friendly people
and for all those in whom I can see your Spirit at work.
Thank you for the people who inspire me to love you better.
And, above all, thank you for coming into this world as a person
                                      yourself,
living and dying for us and our salvation,
O God! At this point I would like to spend a few moments of
                                      not doing anything
but just being in your presence and realizing what you did for me.
O my Lord, especially when I think of your death upon the Cross,
I feel very ashamed.
Because I and all these nice people whom I love around me,
                                      we all put you there.
And we continue to keep you there, so to speak—
no, I know, not literally, but like it is said in Hebrews about
                                      people,
Who "Crucify the Son of God afresh and put him to an open
                                      shame"
Well, what else can we say about all of us,
who profess ourselves your followers and don't have your concern?
Lord, Lord, forgive us;
forgive us, purge our hearts and give us the courage and goodness
of your Holy Spirit to change our complacency.
And here again, let me be quiet a while.

Dear and Holy Lord!
Do give us vision, without which we perish.
I feel I can do very little.
But I must begin. But how, where?
Literacy?
Of encouraging better dietary habits anong the sweepers, etc.,
                  whom I know?
"If any man lacks vision, let him ask in faith, without wavering
                  and it shall be given to him!"
My God is able to supply all
needs—including that of guidance
                  and enough time.

And I believe that these are your promises and so they are true.
O Lord, help me not to waver.
I see before me the mountains of all those problems we've been
                thinking about these last few days.
And my faith is pitifully small by comparison.
Lord, help my unbelief!
(Dear God, how stupid this all looks written down;
it's not meant for writing, this is praying. . . .)
Lord, inspire all of us and let us so be drawn to you
that we will go out in your strength to do your work.
What joy there is in being aware of your presence, O Lord!
Help us to spread that joy and so feed bodies and souls.
O blessed and glorious Lord, God forever and ever!

And at the same time, O Lord, give us urgency.

Things go from bad to worse so quickly,
and also the things we read about pollution almost suggest
that your beautiful and wonderful world is on the verge
         of self-destruction by our "Progress."
Lord, if it is your will, let our economic policies give room for conservation of and responsibility to the things, as well as the
                  people around us.
O God, what a mess we are all in!
But I believe that all things work together for good to them
                  that love you.
Raise up more people to love you and work with you.
Amen, Come, Lord Jesus!

"Personal Prayer" made by the participants of the "School on Worship"

The primary purpose of prayer is not to make requests but to praise, to sing, to chant.
Because the essence of prayer is a song, and man cannot live without a song.

Prayer may not save us. But it may make us worthy of being saved. God needs our help. He cannot do the job alone, because He gave us freedom. And by each deed we do, we either retard or accelerate the coming of redemption.

What's really important is life as a celebration.

—Abraham Heschel, *Intellectual Digest*

The earth's goods
must be divided fairly
and this right of every man
to a just share comes first,
even the right to private property,
and the right to free enterprise,
must yield to justice,

Those who have money,
cannot just spend as they please,
or speculate,
regardless of the way
that others are affected.

The laity must act,
using their initiative,
not waiting for instructions.
The laity must take
the Christian spirit
into the minds and hearts of men,
into morality and laws,
into the structures of society.
The laity must breathe
the spirit of the Gospel
into the changes and reforms
that have to come.

Pope Paul VI: "This is Progress." Easter 1967, © Catholic Institute for International Relations. Reprinted with permission.

Dear God,
Church is alright but you could sure use better music. I hope this does not hurt your feeling. Can you write some new songs?
                  Your friend
                  Barry.

Eric Marshall & Stuart Hampie: *Children's Letters to God*. Copyright by and reprinted with permission of Collins Publishers.

A Clutch Of Song

From Persia
O See How Illusive

Paraphrase:

This short life will be like carving on water; every appearance and degree from the point of view of Wisdom is a mirage. In everything we see there is mortality and destruction. Oh, the One who is ever with you (i.e., God) be with us.

Whoever flees is with you. From evil promptings and suggestions of evil, near You I take refuge. Except You there is no true guide in Good and Bad. O God of Mercy be with us.

If You are my friend I have no fear of the enemy. Where is the fear of events and the bitterness of sorrow? If I spend my life with You it is good. Oh Friend, go not away, come to our sides.

Paraphrase from the Persian by James Laster.

(Note: Make your own paraphrase from this one to fit the music.)

From Vietnam

Con Xóm Làng

Nguyen-Duc-Quang

The following song, a modern song composed by Nguyen-Duc-Quang, is a popular illustration of the theme of rural development, a dominant theme in the pacification program.

THE CHERISHED CHILDREN OF OUR HAMLETS AND VILLAGES

We want to voice our attachment for our villages and hamlets,
Our veneration for our old mothers,
Our love for the flocks of little children.
We want to be true villagers,
The cherished children of our villages and hamlets.
We shall dig new wells,
We shall clear the forest,
We shall reclaim wastelands,
We shall rebuild new homes,
We shall open new roads.

There are Numerous Strings

Text: Rabindranath Tagore
Music: Christopher Coelho, O.F.M.

LEADER: There are nu-mer-ous strings in your lute, let me add my own a-mong them. {ASSEMBLY REPEATS.}

1. Then when you smite your chords, my heart will break its si-lence and my heart will be one with your song.

2. A-midst your num-ber-less stars let me place my own lit-tle lamp.

3. In the dance of your fes-ti-val of lights my heart will throb and my life will be one with your smile.

Let's Grow

Jan Landis

1. We live in tough and tragic times — too bad, too bad.
   The days are filled with tragic things — so sad, so sad.
   While some are satisfied and filled, so many more are starved and chilled — too bad, too bad!

2. We live in worlds so far apart — too bad, too bad!
   The East, the West, the North and South — so sad, so bad!
   With friends it's easy to be kind, but strangers still are strange, we find — too bad, so sad!

3. We live with fears of many kinds — too bad, too bad!
   of body, spirit and the mind — so sad, so sad!
   Instead of loving as we should, we hate and fear and do no good — too bad, so bad!

4. But there's no need to give up hope — I know, I know!
   for men can change within their souls — it's so, it's so!
   The God who set us on this earth
   made us like him and gave us worth — I know, it's so!

5. So we must try to change and grow — I know, I know!
   to rise above the pain, and grow — it's so, it's so!
   Lord, make us glad the world is near
   and give us faith to drive out fear — let's go, let's grow!

Ama Xhe Sha

Moshe Sephula

High-life tempo

A ma xhe sha ham bi le___, a ma xhe sha ham bi le___
It is la-ter than you think___; it is la-ter than you think

___, a ma xhe sha ham bi le___, zi tcho
___, it is la-ter than you think___; so says

___ i ti cha la___! A ma
___ the wea-ther man___! It is

© 1970 Galliard Ltd.

63

Helpful Resources

Heavy Hymns, songs by Ed Summerlin, texts by Roger Ortmayer (Carol Stream, Ill.: Agape), 1972.

New Songs of Asian Cities, I-to Loh, editor (Tainan, Taiwan: Tainan Theological College), 1972. An excellent collection of new songs, with music, from most of the Asian countries.

Risk, quarterly of the World Council of Churches, Geneva, Switzerland. Often has articles, occasionally portions of liturgies, prayers, from different sections of the world ecumenical movement.

Salvation Today and Contemporary Experience (Geneva: World Council of Churches), n.d.

Sing Again, Africa!, Moshe Sephula (Norfolk, England: Galliard Ltd.), 1970. Twelve South African urban folk songs.

Sing a New Song, published by St. Catherine's Home in Andheri, Bombay.

Worship in Youth's Idiom, Gerwin van Leeuwen, editor (Bangalore, India: Christian Centre Publication), 1971-1973. The most useful collection of experimental worship forms available from Asia.